Fame Costs

(A true story of the author's struggle to break into print)

By the same author:

Dew on My Feet
Pimbo
What Pimbo Did Next
Pimbo and Jenny in Old Cambridge
Knock on Any Door
From Cambridge – One and All!
In the Shadow of King's
Gentle Tales of Old Cambridge
Cambridge Tales of Mystery and Mirth
The Magic Book for Cats
Cambridge – As War Clouds Roll By
"A Cambridge Childhood" – (Pimbo and Jenny in the 1920s)

Fame Costs

(A true story of Pimbo's struggle to break into print)

F. T. Unwin

First published in Great Britain, 1987

ISBN 0 9512545 0 2
Published by F. T. Unwin, 9 Cockcroft Place,
Cambridge.
Tel: Cambridge (0223) 352438

Printed and bound by
The Burlington Press (Cambridge) Limited,
Foxton, Cambridge CB2 6SW
Tel: Cambridge (0223) 870266

Drawings by Richard Jakins, 23 Thornton Road,
Girton, Cambridge

PREFACE

A true story of the author's struggle to break into print. It lays bare the whole gamut of the writing trade. Rejection slips, Writers' Circles, Correspondence, Writing Schools, Publishers (good and bad), Booksellers, problems of cash flow. But the author hasn't forgotten the human touch. He takes you round as he visits his customers door-to-door, and tells of how, so far, he has sold 80,000 copies of the books he has written. A must for the aspiring writer!

CONTENTS

CHAPTER 1

The Beginner

Becoming an author, is the aim of countless women, saddled with the burden of bringing up a family, but, staring dreamily, through the kitchen window, hoping, one day for their name, in large letters, to be displayed in a book-seller's window. But, as in a recent T.V. series, the answer is in two words – 'Fame-costs'!

My first attempt at writing a story, was at school, in a small village outside Cambridge, that of Bottisham. I had a young girl, lost in the jungle, about to be attacked by a ferocious tiger; with the tiger in mid-air, I suddenly realised "How was I to save her from such peril?" So I invented a storm, had the lightning strike a tree, which came crashing down onto the blood-thirsty beast, thus, saving the pretty damsel!

Mr Morgan, the headmaster, liked my effort, and sent the story through to each classroom, to be read out aloud by the teacher, thus, unwittingly, setting me along the heart-breaking road to literary fame!

Years later, having come safely through the Second World War, I began a serious attempt to cash in on my pretty dubious school-day success – and become a writer.

A small advertisement in "The Listener" caught my eye. "Literary Agent requires manuscripts for Canadian periodicals. Good rates of pay warranted. Send to: Donald Craig, Literary Agent, Thurles, Lancs."

So out poured all my pent-up literary "genius"; rattling up a story, I couldn't get to the post-box quickly enough. Back came the reply "Dear Mr Unwin, Your manuscript came duly to hand. It is excellent! I shall be sending it to the leading Canadian Journals, and expect its immediate acceptance. Before this can be done, however, please forward 10/-, this amount being my usual fee. Yours sincerely, Donald Craig."

Ten shillings, in the 1947 era, was a substantial amount, but to the starry-eyed, would-be-author, such as myself – no problem! And so it went on, plenty of Ten Shilling postal orders, bags of "Excellent work", "This should sell" – but no sign of success, until, at last I realised that to become a real author, one had to have talent, the question was "Had I got it?"

One thing, friends, relatives, and near kin, do you no good at all. "I think it's lovely", "I've read worse than that in lots of papers", never a hint of real criticism. Criticism, is a vital ingredient in the budding authors' curriculum. So I turned to the correspondence courses. Once again, combing through "The Listener's" literary supplement, I came across: "The British School of Journalism, invites new writers. Earn while you learn. Your work will be supervised by professional authors.

Twenty lessons, in your own time, followed by *real* authors' advice. Reasonable terms. Send for our brochure, and read genuine testimonials from our satsified clients. British School of Journalism, London, W.C.1."

In no time I was at it again! Reams, and reams, of untutored writing. In between, short exercises on dialogue, suspense, descriptive work, drama, comedy. The exercises were well supervised, with sensible advice, bringing out a renewed confidence in my quest to become an author – but once again things went wrong!

Writer-beginners usually make the same mistakes, each thinking their own little crow the blackest. *Their* brain-child beyond criticism. They churn out paper-miles of unpunctuated, non-paragraphed "gems", of nothing more, than a series of events, linked together, without depth, or semblance of a beginning – middle – and end. I was sending off to the writing school, fool-scap material as such, without even making sure that the pages were clipped, and *not* folded.

Although well satisfied with the supervision of my exercises, I found my story material was being returned, folded over, as sent. Footnotes gave me glowing acknowledgements, but, in between, there were no comments, nothing deleted, still unpunctuated. I suddenly suspected that my work had *not* been read, it seemed that the short exercise markings, were meant to keep me sweet – the rest could go by the board.

My doubts went further. The brochure boasted that real authors would review my work, it dawned on me, whether active authors could spare the time away from their own grind-stone, in order to help pure amateurs?

After ten lessons of a scheduled twenty, feeling I was getting nowhere, I left the course. Perusing through a list of other correspondence courses, I found that the British School of Journalism was a tag adopted by several schools, making it very difficult to find a reputable one. Musing over the results of my correspondence course, I put it to myself! Was it that the tutors, realised my short comings as a writer, knowing, that after a few more lessons, they would be rid of me for ever, they would opt out; making any criticisms of my story writing, maybe, as a kindness to myself, I was just plain nuts – and should give up thinking of myself as a writer!

With the traditional tendency of the beginner, never taking no for an answer, and thinking it wasn't me, it was the others; I embarked on an orgy of short story writing; armed with the Author's and Artist's Yearbook, I picked out a list of potential editorials, sending out, one after the other, to the hapless publishers.

Robert Louis Stevenson, had a reputation of receiving enough rejection slips to paper his bed-room, I must have out-done him by scores and scores.

When the flap of the letter-box clicks, you sense immediately your fate. Should it be a heavy enough 'plop', it means your manuscript has been returned. The would-be-author, is always waiting for the slim envelope, just a light 'plop' on the mat, or hall 'lino, with the cheque, and a request for more of your work!

At times, rejection-slips contain a comely piece of advice, to spur on those, whom, the Editor feels have enough talent to make the grade. But, in the main, rejection-slips seem like a stab in the back – so far, I had not received a rejection-slip offering any iota of hope.

However, from my course experiences I *was* learning: it was prudent to send a covering note to the Editor, wise, to study the type of reader the Journal catered for. A copy of the "Author's and Artist's" was a must, it gave the address of all Journals, inland and abroad, the length of the material involved, payment, you could say, it was the author's bible!

One day, my luck changed! I had written a story about a young coloured immigrant, who had been adopted by a British family. At school, he came under a barrage of insults, and was having a very unhappy time. Accusations of thieving, exacerbated the lad's troubles, and although innocent, he was on the verge of being sent to an approved school. With the memory of my having extricated the young girl in the jungle from an equally tight spot; I conjured up a likely ending, by having the lad do a sacrificial act of bravery at a fire in the school, saving many of the pupils; with one of the rescued pupils owning up to the theft, of which the coloured boy had been accused!

It didn't sell – but it was a near miss!

The "rejection-slip", thanked me for my contribution, pointing out, that owing, to the racist aspect of my story, I had failed to convince a committee of seven – by the odd vote! It was during the early days of coloured immigrants coming into the country. Apparently, some narrow minded person was not quite ready for such innovations, although, years later, the situation changed completely.

Somehow I felt I was on my way!

However, it wasn't to be, although fired with a new enthusiasm by the near miss, the rejection slips still kept coming in, even to the extent of evoking a wry smile from the postman!

Came a small consolation! My local paper offered a prize for the best contribution concerning the readers' vocation, anecdotes, or funny happenings during working hours were invited. At the time, I was working as a milkman, which afforded me bags of material for entry. I came second, in a batch of several hundred entries, which, once again, gave me the impetus to keep going with my writing!

In between failures, I swotted up on every aspect of the writing trade. Oh, yes, many an article expounded the bitterness and rejection traumas of the "Long Distance Short-Story Writer". In one article, I read of a Mr Ross, an American Journalist, who, out to prove the difficulties that beset the beginner, did the following: He typed out, in manuscript form, a novel which a few years previously, had received rave notices. Selecting six well known publishers, and two literary agents, he sent a manuscript to each, on the assumption that he was a budding author. Of the eight manuscripts, three were lost, four returned with curt rejection slips, one returned by a literary agent, offered a semblance of hope, but, adding a rider 'that he was prepared to do a little revision on the work!'

Another Journalist, a Mr Perry, doing a survey for an elite literary magazine, on a similar theme to that of Mr Ross, on behalf of the beginner-writer, achieved the following: he analysed four published short stories, studied the characters, and plots intently, then carefully changed the names of characters, switched the settings of the stories, but in context, style, and narrative form, kept rigidly to the story line, it was just as though he was doing a 'Tom Keating', instead of painting fakes, he produced an exact replica of four short stories!

These, he sent out to various magazines – not one sold, just two rejection-slips offering a small solace of revision.

All this, to show how difficult it was for a new author to break into print, almost, suggesting that an element of luck is needed in most acceptances. Editors, too, sent in articles, pointing out that on an average, three-hundred manuscripts reached their desks almost every day. At the first sign of the amateur writer – into the waste paper bin it went (especially those with no covering note, or S.A.E.) In regard to the publication of a book, the cost of producing two or three hundred bound volumes, was in the region of three thousand pounds; taking everything into account! The publisher could not afford to take chances on an unknown writer, he wanted his money back for the initial outlay.

Well aware that I'd taken on a hard, heart breaking task, in order to break into print, I was lucky in that I had behind me a wife with complete faith in my ability to do just that. Jenny had stuck to me through thick and thin. We were living in Cherry Hinton at the time, my job being that of a milkman.

House to house selling

One day, during my correspondence-course sessions, I could see her approaching me from the Mill Road area, I was in the middle of my milk round. She seemed excited, and had caught the bus from Cherry Hinton especially for the occasion.

Handing me a printed letter, she stood back expectantly!

It was from my course Tutor. "Dear Mr Unwin, This is your best work, so far. It is realistic, has a topical flavour, plenty of suspense and conflict. You have shown marked improvement in your work. I suggest you submit this manuscript to the 'London Evening News' or 'The London Evening Standard'. I'm positive that you are on a winner! Best wishes, V G Richardson."

The note's main message, was typed in red ink, and had been sent *outside* the course's usual procedures.

I gave Jenny a hug and kiss, irrespective of my customer's curtain adjustments!

During the early post-way days, accommodation was very hard to come by. Consequently, unscrupulous landlords were taking advantage of young couples desperate for living quarters. My story, was about such like activities, the particular landlord had over charged, and rented out a rat infested hovel. The young husband, with a small child, had gone into her bedroom to kiss her goodnight – a large rat jumped from the bed! With, Peter Rachman, in mind. . . . .

The young man went beserk! Sorting out the landlord and giving a vehement mouthful to the housing authorities, who had condoned such lettings. This gave me plenty of space in which to consolidate my drama, conflict, suspense, and dialogue exercises – in short, "I'd gone to town".

Watching my wife's happy face, and her, "Look's like you cracked it, at last!" was a very special bonus. I could almost hear the slim envelope dropping onto the mat as silently as a snowflake. The postman's wry smile, turned into one of sharing my triumph. Above all, Jenny's faith in me had paid dividends – I was on my way at last.

But, it wasn't to be! Despite sending the story out to most of the London papers, a few journals, it was the same old rejection slips, none with any hope, and I was back to square one.

Even then, Jenny still held out hope. "Give them time. They have a lot to go through you know, your's isn't the only one!"

I had visions of my manuscripts being at the bottom of the three hundred, piled on an over worked Editor's desk. But I felt for Jenny. Her spirits had risen high since the Tutor's acclaim of my work. I wanted more than anything to succeed, just to give *her* a special bonus.

The current course I was on, was coming to its conclusion. Although being satisfied with the way it had dealt with my efforts – I still had failed to register a "hit". One day, going through my usual perusals of the literary pages, I spotted an alluring advertisement, it read: "New writers needed! We guarantee that course fees will be repaid to you, should you not earn enough through your published work, to pay for the enrolment. We market your work! Write: Writers' Ring, Clun, Shropshire."

This seemed to be it! I had worked hard, for four solid years, I'd written reams, and reams, long hand, at that! Every day, either Jenny, or I, had waited expectantly for that elusive slim envelope. Being unable to type, I had paid pounds for the preparations of my manuscripts. So, I became a pupil at the Writers' Ring school of journalism, the cost, twenty pounds for a twenty lesson course.

The first package I received was disappointing. The correspondence dealing with the writing side of the course, seemed to have been run off on a Gestetner machine, on very cheap paper, at that! A surprise item was a month's supply of "a plot for everyday". On perusal, I found little inspiration from them, they seemed too contrived. But, little did I know of the very tough time I was embarking upon!

CHAPTER 2

A Glimmer of Hope

My first lesson from the Writers' Ring, was similar to that of the British School of Journalism. The exercise was on descriptive work. "Give a descriptive account of a large black dog emerging from the sea on a lovely summer day". My reply was as follows:

The beautiful collie, with its black form contrasting magically with the golden sands, stood statue-like, as he shook the sea water from his body. A silver cascade of sea-spray, intermingling with the shimmering heat rays, gave off a whirligig of a kaleidoscopic eidos form colour. The tide, ebbed, as though desirous of affording the dog a larger stage.

Smugly, I thought, this should get me off to a flying start. But, once again, I was in for disappointment, the story to follow, was pulled to bits.

My story was bespattered with a red pencil across a good many pages. "Trite", "Rubbish", "Unconvincing", "Characters have no depth", "You must tie up the loose ends". A word I used frequently was "situation", in the context of "What do you think of the situation?" My tutor blasted me for this. "*What* situation? You *must* explain, not use such woolly phrases. You are taking short cuts, and cheating the readers. Another thing! You're plucking characters out of thin air, with no depth, you must introduce the character earlier, during some stage of the story".

And so it went on! Although pleased, that at least, I *was* getting criticism, it made me wonder whether I really was up to a writer's standard. Getting good marks for exercise work, was like a short sprinter unable to go a fuller distance.

My following work was in keeping with the Tutor's remarks, I must have been trying too hard!

"Far too wooden!" came the marked version. "You are writing as though I'm standing behind you, try to be more natural. You must learn to take criticism in a positive manner. Constructive criticism is, to a beginner, the life blood of a writer to be. Remember too, that a writer is presenting to his readership, a world stage of real live characters; they are in the foreground – *you*, as a writer must stay in the background!"

So, away I went again! Trying, as I thought, to be more natural. My marked work was returned – as *almost* a tragedy!

As I have stated before, Jenny was behind me all the way. My daughter, Christine, though only eleven, looked upon me as a future writer of books. My son, Keith, had a great sense of humour, also, he loved to tease. We had a rather strange mutual understanding with each other, in that, should there be a letter for me unopened,

Keith made no bones about reading its contents; he would leave the open letter, in a prominent place for me to view on my return from work. By looking at my son's face, I knew whether or not, I'd made a sale, or received good marks from the Writers' Ring. On this particular day, Keith viewed me with almost contempt. "Why don't you pack it up dad, you're making a fool of yourself." I reached out for the letter!

"Dear Mr Unwin – Your recent work, was so bad, that I had the unusual task of looking up your course membership number, to ascertain that this work actually came from you. It was far below your usual talent. I must say at once, that you *have* shown promise, but, perhaps you are getting a little stale. Sometimes, an author gets bogged down on a story, we call it "going stale on you". Now, I suggest that you put this particular story aside, forget about it, go back to it at a later date. You are in a position, of that, of an amateur pilot, whose plane has crashed, but leaving him unhurt. Should he not get back into the air, quickly, he may never fly again! I want you to send me a story, 1,200 words, write it to suit the "Christian Herald" Journal. I know you can do it! Best wishes, Your Tutor, Writers' Ring.

Although, my initial reaction to the letter was one of bitter disappointment, I felt that the Tutor deserved a medal, for taking such an interest in me. No one, so far, had given me encouragement to such a degree. Somehow, I felt that this time, I mustn't let him down, I'd keep going until I did get it right! Looking up the usual stories in the Christian Herald, I found they liked simple stories, not, as one might think of a Journal with a Christian title, but everyday stories with a leaning toward the "decent" thing. Also, they had a special corner for the teenager, depicting the problems of leaving school, getting a job, and such like. So that was it! A story about a young boy.

On my way to Sawston, a small village outside Cambridge, I had spotted at the foot of a bridge, a small fairy like cottage, named "Dingle Dell". It was sunk deeply in a hollow, barely discernible from the road, surrounded by a small thicket. It seemed to me a perfect setting for a little boy to explore and have adventures.

So, I had the boy drop in unexpectedly at the picturesque cottage, I gave the little dwelling, roses around the door, sparrows twittering under the wire-mesh of the pretty thatched roof. Its occupant, a dear little gnome-like gentleman, sporting a Father Christmas beard, was a toy-maker, in the Pinnocchio style. The boy, and he, "clicked" almost on first sight. The old gentleman taught the lad all he knew about toy-making, in a short while, the boy become almost as efficient as the old craftsman.

The boy, was regarded at school, as a bit of a duffer. The teachers showed him little respect, even his parents were a little disappointed in their only son's progress. Just before the end of the Christmas Term, the children were asked to bring along anything they had made, for a Christmas Fayre, in aid of school funds.

Teachers, and parents, the whole school, were amazed at the workmanship of the toys the school duffer had brought along. They were the pride of the Fayre, and the boy was feted for his artistic creation, enjoying a respect he had never known before – with a fine future as a toy-maker, much to the delight of his parents. I called the story "Miracle at Dingle Dell".

The reply from my Tutor, got me all excited!

Dear Mr Unwin – A short story of 1,200 words, is little more than a spotlight, on a certain theme. Just a glimpse, as it were. There is no room for meanderings, too much descriptive work, or fringe characters. The story must move quickly to the finish, or denouement. However, I find that you have made the work, a 1,400 word job, you must be more careful about this, as it can be the difference between acceptance and rejection. I have good news for you – take out two hundred words, and I believe the story could be sold. Best wishes, your ever-patient Tutor.

I could hardly believe it! Scanning through the story over and over again, taking out two hundred words was proving to be a difficult decision, as to which paragraphs had to go. In the end, it had to be the "twittering sparrows under the wire mesh of the little thatched cottage." Also, "the roses around the door, and the sun that came peeping in at noon!"

Beginners, I was finding out, had a tendency, to over-do things in the description aspect. It seemed that we tried too hard to sublimate our shortcoming, by showing off, it got you nowhere in the acceptance stakes! So out came two hundred words of "Miracle at Dingle Dell".

Working very hard in the following weeks, with a lingering ear for the letter-box click, I had almost given up hope – when it happened!

Returning home from work, I found the slim brown envelope lying opened on the table. Keith, for once, did not meet my eye, he sat with his head turned away. Looking at the back of the envelope, I read "Christian Herald", even then, I wondered – was that it?

The two old ladies at the theatre

It was! My years of slogging away long hand, the disappointments, the hope that one day I might make it – the letter read: "Dear Mr Unwin, We have accepted your manuscript, for publication. We shall be forwarding you a complimentary copy of the edition containing your story. Payment, £2 2s, will be made on the day of publication. We look forward to the acceptance of more of your work. However, we must add a rider to the contract. The title must be changed to that of "Miracle at the Copse", we hope you will fall in with the alterations. Best wishes, The Editor"

For a moment, I was perplexed as to why the title needed changing. Then, the penny dropped – the title of the current hit song was "My Little Ding-a-ling". It seemed that the paper deemed the title must too suggestive for a family Journal. To be honest, I couldn't have cared less what they called it, I would have written back, and agreed to be put in the stocks for a fortnight!

Finishing the letter, I found Keith laughing with me, at the turn of events. "You've cracked it, dad. I never thought you would, well done dad!"

Jenny, was making a cup of tea in celebration. Christine, just back from school, was all over me "wait until I tell the girls at school, my dad's a *real* author!"

My wife laughed. We had often discussed the position of the writer who kept the pulp magazines busy with copy. Were they real writers? The brochure of the British School of Journalism, pointed out that stories in the Women's Journals, were in the main, written by housewives, who had mastered the art of story-writing for the mass of lonely "housebounds", searching for love and romance through the written word.

But, then again, a guest writer, Beverley Nichols, had pointed out, that it was just as difficult to write a story about a "Servant girl in the Red Star weekly, as one for an elite magazine as Argosy".

I was smiling at the payment of two guineas for my work. It had cost £1 for typing, and had I charged for the revision, and time taken in writing – well!

But I was *so* delighted. Now, I was a published author in my own right. I couldn't thank the Tutor enough, I just couldn't fathom out why he had shown such a marked interest in *me* – was it a vicarious attempt, to reflect back on his own hard slog, before *his* making the grade?

At that time, I had changed jobs. I was now a hostel keeper at a hostel run by Kings College. Part-time, that is, because Jenny, was actually running the hostel, and my new vocation was that of a psychiatric nurse at Fulbourn Hospital.

Further delight was to come my way. On receiving my cheque, and free copy, on the day of publication from the Christian Herald: not only was my story featured in a prominent place in the Journal, it has also been illustrated: I felt as proud as a peacock, that some artist would be commissioned to work on a story written by 'yours truly!'

There, in the centre of the story, stood my brainchild, taking in the old man's pixie-like cottage, amazingly, the artists had captured every salient point of the two characters, as though he had written it himself.

All this doubled by efforts towards more success. To me, it seemed like learning to drive a car, the gears in a hopeless muddle, the dense traffic problems, the road-sense to master. Then, suddenly the gears drop into place, almost automatically, the road seems wider, pedestrians less of a Jay-walking problem – hey presto, I'm a writer, but where was I going?

During the course of three months, I had written three more short stories, these, had been accepted by various Journals. To prove to myself that I could manage on my own, I sent another off, on my own bat. This, I despatched to the Journal that had turned me down by one vote – to my joy, it was accepted.

Taking stock of my progress, I had earned the colossal sum of ten guineas, for an outlay of fifty pounds or more, not accounting for my typing expenses. But, you can take it from me, that I was still more than satisfied with my successes – but, somehow, I must go off on a different tangent!

I found that magazines, women's Journals, were getting inundated with stacks of manuscripts. One Journal, having accepted my story, kept me waiting fourteen-months before publication and payment. Having written to enquire the reason for the delay, I was curtly told that, "mine was steadily climbing to the top". Another journal explained that stories were placed into categories, romance, drama, comedy, and so forth. I also learned that rejection, in some cases, was not always made because of sub-standard work, merely, that the particular type of story, had dozens of similar ones awaiting publication.

My course with the Writers' Ring had terminated. Feeling confident that I would be able to strike out on my own, I wrote a very special letter of appreciation to the Tutor. It seemed as though he had been a father to me. I'm positive that without his marvellous help and patience, I would never have seen my work in print.

Browsing over my old lessons, the exercises, the criticisms, I had gained a great deal of expertise. It seemed, amazing to me, that would-be-writers, without experience, would spend hours and hours at their desks, receive rejection-slip after rejection-slip, and still not realise that something was missing! I'm sure, that the same person, would not take his watch to pieces, and expect to put it back perfectly!

I remember the Tutor telling me to pretend, that I was sitting behind a couple of dear old ladies at the theatre, watching a play, which was no "great shakes". "Isn't he like my youngest, nephew, dear?" One might say. The other replies "I was just going to say the same dear – but I think he's a little fatter in the face!"

Then, would follow a repartee concerning the type of dresses worn by the ladies in the play, colour of the curtains, "Just like Agatha's – remember dear?" and so it would go on.

The Tutor told me to have a large notice on my writing desk. "Make a scene of it!" Don't give the reader time to digress. When being carried away by a descriptive paragraph, think of the two old ladies, put some action into it." It made me smile at the mistakes I'd made:

- Sending off stuff with no S.A.E.
- Writing manuscripts, with no margins for corrections.
- Choosing a magazine, such as Blackwoods, then send off a story more suitable for "Peg's Own Paper"
- Using rejected material for other Journals, without sprucing up the top cover, so that it arrived with a very jaded appearance.
- Failing to appreciate criticism during the early days, on the strength, that, I knew best!

Jenny put it to me one morning, "Why don't you write a book. There'd be more money in it, after all, you've been through a hard apprenticeship, I think you can do it?"

This point had struck me before. It was a far cry from a 1,200 word effort – writing a full length book! I remembered the brochure saying, most stories in the womens' Journals were written by housewives. Was it a different kettle-of-fish? Without taking anything away from such type of writing, *could* I reach a higher level.

I realised too, that to the established writer, writing a short story for "Harper's Magazine" was a work of art, compared to my puny efforts in the pulp Journals.

Jenny knew me well! "Now come off it. You're as good as the next, that's your trouble – never think you're good enough! I've peeped in some of the so called best-sellers, every other page – a load of filth. There must be thousands of readers that don't like pornography, as a reading diet!"

Nodding in appreciation, I made up my mind. I'd write an autobiographical novel of my life. I was an illegitimate, had suffered from T.B., and was brought up in the poverty stricken days of the post-war era of the 'twenties'. I'd bring in all the old characters, I could use as much padding as I wished, even the old ladies in the theatre, would be excused for the meanderings. My nickname was "Pimbo" – that's it, I'd call the book "Pimbo".

CHAPTER 3

Pimbo

My success with the short stories, had made me a little impatient to get on with my plans to write a book. Jenny, bless her, had pointed out the pitfalls. Would my boyhood be of real interest to the public? Had my childhood been too bland, was it not a fact that the same things had happened to so many others. Could I find a publisher willing to take it on?

Jenny was right in her questioning, it *was* all for my benefit. But, I too, had given much thought to the matter, and had come up with: I was born in the back streets of Cambridge, knew every sleazy alley-way in the Kite area of the City. Being curious about life, I'd pushed my neck into every conceiveable aspect of poverty. When old characters met at the corner of the street, I stopped to listen. I even crept into houses, sat underneath the dining table, listening to the family quarrels. Then too, I had travelled around with my dad on his rag and bone round, met everyone from farmer to tied-cottage labourer.

Also, the book, actually, would be about people, and the way of life in those far-off days. As the

Writers' Ring has taught me, *I* was to be in the background, presenting a host of characters, myself, as an incidental feature.

An article in the local paper had caught my eye. John Gaskell, the Cambridge Evening News Journalist-Reporter had just completed a survey on books, and writers. It was found that an author was quite content with a sale of 400 hard-backs. The book trade was in such a state that most book-shops were offering sale-or-return facilities only, with a severe cut-down on books taken on – in some cases three – six, appeared to be the "order of the day!"

A nagging doubt, was, could I really come up with the goods? In Heffers' window, were pictures of well known authors with their latest offerings. A time, and day, when they would be visiting the shop to autograph their work. Somehow, I couldn't really visualise myself in such an illustrious position. But, against this, an article concerning book-shops, had appeared in the Spectator. It told of a bookshop in London, with three-tier departments, on a certain occasion, with the author waiting patiently at the table, finding very few takers.

The manager, arranged, that staff from each department, would take turns in arriving at the author's table, even to the extent of changing top clothing, this giving an illusion of a busy turnover.

Then again, how would I conduct myself at interviews. I was the type of chap, that arriving at an office for an interview with the boss, would be told by a haughty receptionist, "You can't leave your cycle against the window, you know!" or "I hope you haven't left your lorry outside – there's parking restrictions, you know!"

With my experiences on the milk round, I found hundreds of housewives, who relished the thought of becoming authors. "I could write a book on all that my dear old dad told me about his childhood!" they'd say. "According to my dear old mum, there used to be some *right* old characters living around here – if only I could put pen to paper!"

Many letters from women, displayed in the agony columns of the weekly pulps, showed a wonderful sense of human emotions, comedy, and hidden talent for telling a story. Writing short pieces, however, was far different from novel writing. But, I reckoned, given the chance, hundreds of potential authors, sat trapped in their homes, waiting for the kids to come home from school, might well blossom into a Barbara Cartland, and write romantic novels to enthrall their contemporaries. Chatting it over with Jenny, we mulled over all the whys and wherefores. We reckoned that the book would be one of some 60,000 words or more. I'd write twenty chapters of a 3,000 word duration. Writers' Ring had taught me to count the words on each line, then multiply by the amount of lines to a page, and ten words per line, thus giving me, give or take a few lines, a three hundred word page, with ten pages per chapter, and twenty chapters making up the book.

My course experience taught me to use foolscap with margins for correction on each side. A point that worried me was how would I react to facing up to finding enough material to cover twenty chapters. I found that, should a certain eccentric character live in the street and a pen picture of him was needed for an article, unless you knew a great deal about him, the words might soon fizzle-out!

Looking up my Writers' Ring lessons, I found answers: concerning the chapter problem – concentrate on *one* chapter at a time. The eccentric characters, embellish around the facts known about him. Then when you have got inside his skin, you can put actions and words into the personality, keep him in the context of his real self, by this method, you are less likely to run out of words.

My Tutor had accentuated on the point. A certain writer had been asked to write an article on a very important wedding. Somehow, he was unable to arrive at the church on time. On making it to the reception, he listened to the gossip and small talk concerning the actual wedding ceremony. Embellishing on all he'd heard, he wrote in, his version of the events at the church. To his surprise, a few days after the appearance of the article in his local press, he received letters praising his account of the ceremony; one lady pointing out "It was just like being there – all over again!"

Motivation for writing a book was no problem. I had come so far along the writers' trail – I couldn't turn back. I'd set my heart on becoming a writer, I owed it to Jenny, who had given me so much support. Then, of course, was the money! Training as a psychiatric nurse, brought in just over nine-pounds per week. Jenny, to tide over the poor wages, until I would be earning more money as a registered nurse, had taken a job as an assistant-nurse.

Then again, reading in a literary magazine, I found that only around five-per-cent of authors, actually earned a living at writing. The rest, used it as a part-time means of improving their income. It was indeed a strange world. Books that won prizes for various literary awards, sometimes sold no more than two hundred copies. They were reviewed in high class glossy periodicals, but, the *ordinary* reader, rarely purchased a copy. Reading on, I found that the prize-winner for the best first-novel-of-the-year, although fêted in the literary journals, sold just 1,000 copies.

On the strength of all this, I daren't expect a great financial return. The self satisfaction of actually writing a book, would be enough – but, it would be a splendid bonus, should I make *some* money. The author of "Porterhouse Blues", Tom Sharpe, told me in the privacy of his kitchen, "Boy, you'll get telephone calls, radio and T.V. interviews. You'll get people calling at the door – but, there'll be *no* money! A film company told me to keep in touch, they might adapt the book into a film. Do you know, I haven't been on holiday for two years – just waiting for the 'great day'!" (Tom eventually made it through "Blott on the Landscape".)

Apart from all these likely set-backs, I started writing "Pimbo" a story of a boyhood in the 1920s. Taking in the fact that I was born in the work-house, my father died in the work-house, embracing the soup kitchens, pawnshops, the 'Sally' Army, and the weird and wonderful characters, that strove against terrible odds, to make their lives a little more tolerable. I was to take my readers into the back streets of the sleazy thoroughfares, enter into the homes of the meanest, and the poor. There would be laughter and tears, boyish pranks, childhood memories, a real pot-pourri of life's emotions.

Working hard at it, I finished the novel in one year. I wrote it long hand, did bags of revisions, then sat back, and wrote it all over again. Often, through the long lonely stint, I would ask myself, "Was it all for nothing?" It wasn't as though I was a carpenter, and had produced a worthwhile piece of furniture. It was something in the abstract, just words on a piece of paper, nothing tangible, and that horrible feeling that it wouldn't catch on. "Watership Down", the "Day of the Jackal" had been turned down by several publishers, what sort of chance would "Pimbo" stand?

I hadn't even the Writers' Ring Tutor to turn to. I thought of Robert Louis Stevenson busily papering his bedroom with rejection-slips.

Jenny cheered me up, "It's good. As good as anything, it's true, it's about real life. You mustn't lose heart, anyway, God will see to it that you haven't worked hard all these years for nothing!"

Christine, my daughter, added strength to her mother's argument. She, with her boy-friend, were very keen on a jazz-group called "The Savoy Jazzmen". They were an excellent group, led by Barry Palser, the lead trumpeter. Playing in the group, in one of his many guises, an expert, and near genius in all he attempted, was Russell Davies, writer, T.V. critic, book reviewer, T.V.

presenter, musician extraordinaire, and theatre critic, and excellent rugby player thrown in for good measure!

Christine promised "I'll take it to Russell, he'll give you a good idea as to its merit. He won't beat about the bush, he'll tell you straight, if he thinks it's no good. You do that dad, then you can take it from there!"

The manuscript was bound, almost into book form, with nice blue edges. With a great deal of trepidation, I handed the work over to my daughter, and awaited the worst!

It came in a large white envelope, separate from the returned manuscript. A letter, and review from such a personage as Russell Davies! I read the review with surprise and delight. He told me to go along with it, pointing out that he saw no reason why it shouldn't succeed. Russell, enjoyed the story, its humour, pathos, and reality. "Pimbo", he thought, was perhaps a little too good to be true, (make him do one or two naughty things, scrumping apples, and the like). He wished me the best of luck on the work, and should I, at a future date, require advice, not to be afraid to ask. Signed, Russell Davies.

I thought it wonderful, that a busy man such as he, would find time to review a book written by a raw beginner. So there it was, a book to be launched upon the unsuspecting public – what was my next move to be?

Once again the Writers' Ring course, came to the rescue. The local paper, should, they suggested, be quite happy to give space to a local author, especially as the theme of the story

1,500 copies of unsold poems

centred around its own environment. I read my lessons over and over again, coming to the conclusion that the Cambridge Evening News would be first to receive my manuscript.

At the same time, I looked several publishers up in the "Author's and Writers" year book, sending off a covering note to each of them.

Taking along with me copies of my short story successes, and a bound copy of Pimbo, I walked tentatively into the News office. Mr John Alexander, showed me into his office. I went through my paces, trying not to miss a trick. I had already made sure of "not leaving my cycle leaning against the window, and had removed my cycle-clips!"

The News editor viewed me a little sceptically. Butting in now, and again, with "But, we don't usually do this sort of thing. Printing costs are going up, you know!"

I stuck to my guns. But, somehow I felt that he was not too keen on me. I had a horrible thought and felt ashamed of it, but, I wondered what would have taken place had I been a College Don, or, some kind of dignitary. In the end, he reached over, took my book from the desk, remarking rather laconically, "Leave it with me, Mr Unwin, I'll see what we can do with it, but don't expect too much!"

So, the weeks went by! Of the publishers I had written to, after a ten-week lapse, I had a reply from Methuen's, a children's book publisher, they would like to publish the manuscript, but point out, that having a two years' waiting list, I would have to wait my turn. Another ten weeks passed by, with a reply from two publishers; each, turning down my offer, each with a similar excuse of a long waiting rota. Of the other three, I received *no* reply, despite my enclosing a S.A.E. During all this hanging in limbo period, I, through various literary Journals, did a little research on publishers!

Sending a manuscript to a publisher, could be very time consuming. Quite easily, a year could elapse before receiving a reply. (Present day authors are advised to get in touch after eight weeks). The publisher might send it out to a very busy "reader", thus prolonging the waiting period. Even on acceptance, it's quite on the cards that the book may never get published. I read a case of one author having written what he intended to be a "series", a kind of "Saint" character, in the Leslie Charteris mould. It was accepted, and the author received an advance-fee. But, for some reason or other, the publisher decided not to put the book into print.

Having paid the advance-fee, it seemed, that the publisher held all the copyright on the book's further publication. The author, anxious to get the book, and a likely series in print, was thwarted at every turn. He sued the publishers; at the moment, the case is in High Court.

In another case, the author, too had received an advance fee, with no hint of publication. A year or so later, on holiday up North, well away from his area, to his surprise, he found copies of his book on sale at a prominent book store.

Sometimes, author's books become "remaindered", which means they are sold off at a greatly reduced price to the booksellers, thus reducing the amount of royalties payment to the author. Some publishers have done this without contacting the writer, who, for the first time, sees his book "in the window, at Sale Price!"

Thankfully, the majority of publishers are good, honest men, who arrange hype-parties to launch a new novel, pay royalties on time, and keep the writer up-to-date on the movement of his book.

By this time, eight months had gone by, since my leaving the "Pimbo" manuscript with the Cambridge Evening News. Experience had taught me not to be too hasty. Pestering the paper, might result in its return to me with a curt rejection note – so I soldiered on. One day, a Mr John Osborne received a write up in the local paper. He was a poet of good standing, who believed in poetry that had something to say in verse form, but, not too much so called modern idiom. To prove his point, he was about to launch a booklet of poems by local authors.

He was asking for contributions, but, in order to present a good looking booklet, accepted poets, would pay £2, on the assumption that should the idea "take off", a second booklet would be marketed, and the fee of £2, would be returned.

A little pen-happy, because of my awaiting news of "Pimbo", I sent off three poems, to my delight, John accepted two of them. The poet had done his homework, most of the book-shops in Cambridge were displaying the booklets in their windows. On reading the poems, I was surprised at the quality of the writers, it made me wonder how on earth mine had been accepted. A month later, John sent all contributors a list of sales, in all, 400 copies had been sold, including those of the Foyle's bookshop in London!

John, immediately started off another booklet, with the expectations, that this time, contributors, not only, *not* having to pay a fee, might even receive payment! But, alas, the project did not prosper. Sales were disappointing, and John was so honest, that he wouldn't allow his poets to start fee-paying again, the whole plan fell through.

The difficulty in making anything out of poetry, unless in the very top bracket, came to my thoughts as I ruefully mulled over John's failure. During my milk round days, a dear lady used to call me in for a cup of tea. One day, she asked me whether or not, I liked poetry. On my affirmation, she went upstairs, bringing down a small well bound book of poems, with her name emblazoned on the cover of the book; "That's for you!" she said sweetly.

Noticing the price inside, five shillings, I offered to pay her something.

"I had two thousand printed, paid for them myself. The publisher told me that they should sell. Upstairs, I must have at least 1,500 copies left. I've been giving them away for the last ten years. My relatives love them, my grand children read them to their teachers in school. I don't mind, really, I got it all off my chest – and managed something I wanted to do all my life – get my name in print!"

Returning home, I read through the book. They were beautiful poems, far better than I could have written. About nature, birds, scenery, lovely kind thoughts from a lovely kind person. But, they didn't sell, in a world that had seen two horrible wars.

With a year gone by, and still no news concerning "Pimbo", I decided to take the bull by the horns and pop into the News office at Newmarket Road, to find out my fate!

CHAPTER 4

Sweet and Sour

Walking along Maids' Causeway on my way to the News building, I thought over the fact, that two years had elapsed since "Pimbo" had been conceived. I began to wonder whether my chances in making the big times would ever come to fruition. I mused over a snippet in the Literary Journal. Competition in the publishing world is very fierce. 52,000 new titles are published every year, of the 3,000 privately owned bookshops in the U.K., half have a turnover of less than £1,000 per week. Before I could get further into the doldrums, I had reached the News offices.

It was a Saturday, the usual goings and comings in the reception lobby were missing. I had quite a long wait after the girl at the desk had phoned Mr Alexander, to say, that Mr Unwin was waiting downstairs.

Eventually, the News boss confronted me. I almost stammered out my request. Had there been any further developments with "Pimbo", it had been well over a year since my bringing the manuscript in, I hoped I wasn't being too hurried?

John Alexander looked surprised, "Oh, oh, I see,

you've come about the "Pimbo" manuscript – I don't think we've done anything yet, we've been very busy you know – would you like to take it back?" The remark stunned me! I could see all my hopes dashed into little pieces. I could almost picture Jenny's face! Would I like to take it back? I expected him to ask, "Was my cycle left leaning against the office windows?"

Talking to the editor of the Cambridge Evening News

It seemed so unbelieveable, I stared at him, my lips moved, but no sound came out. After a few seconds I found myself saying "Well, yes. I may as well!"

He went upstairs again, after at least ten minutes, he returned empty-handed. "I can't lay my hands on it at the moment – we'll return it to you during the week!"

I was getting cross, very cross! Somehow, I didn't care any more, I knew what Jenny would have done, she'd have stormed into the building, demanding then, and there, the manuscript's return. Looking John squarely in the eyes, I said "I'd like it now, please. I'll wait, I don't care how long, but I'll wait. It must be here somewhere, you find it!"

He turned quickly and went back upstairs. It must have been at least fifteen minutes, before he came almost running down the long staircase, holding the blue edged manuscript.

"I'm sorry, it was on Rodney Tibbs desk all the time. Small wonder that I couldn't find it!" He handed it back to me.

As I held the book, something came over me. I wondered what the Writers' Ring Tutor would have advised. Two years work gone by the board, no joy from any of the publishers, I was back to square one!

For Jenny's sake, for the Tutor's sake, and the little bit of pride I had left in me, I handed it back to the News Man.

"Oh, well, I'll let you keep it. Perhaps Mr Tibbs hasn't read it yet, maybe he has plans for it!"

Mr Alexander, took back the book without

further argument. To his immense credit, he also smiled. “Oh, all right then, I’m sorry about the delay, we’ll call you should anything develop!”

On the way back, I visualised “Pimbo” being read by first one reporter, then another. I counted up the days one might have taken to read it, perhaps loaned it to the next door neighbour. Bringing it back for the perusal of the next in turn. All this time, I was sat, waiting for news of the outcome. A whole year had gone by with no-one bothering to tell me anything, maybe, it would have gone round and round for ever, from one desk to another, who knows, had I not intercepted the circuit, it would be doing the rounds still?

By the time I reached home, I’d cooled down somewhat. I didn’t tell Jenny everything, just there *could* be hope yet, Mr Tibbs had it on his desk!

Jenny almost laughed, “I hope he hasn’t had it on his desk for a whole year. The poor old cleaner must have got fed up with picking it up, and putting it down!” You couldn’t kid my Jenny, I swear she knew all the time!

In a more serious vein, Jenny asked me why the manuscript had been kept so long without any comment on its merit, did I think the News were stalling, had John Alexander accepted it back out of kindness, later, to return it by post, with the usual rejection?

Somehow, I hadn’t the heart to make any suggestion, I’d been through so many ifs, and buts. The answer came six weeks later, starting with a tap at the door.

"I'm John Gaskell, the News reporter. I've been assigned to write a series on "Pimbo". We intend to do an excerpt once a week, for a six weeks duration!" explained the slim bespectacled young man.

Jenny, and I couldn't, believe it, we almost pinched each other, to make sure it wasn't a dream after all.

The young journalist, went on, "I've read the book, and thoroughly enjoyed it, I thought it smashing, I'd like to take a few particulars, on your experiences as a writer – a kind of introduction to the series. By the way, Mr Petty at the Reference Library of Cambridgeshire Past Memories, is to supply us with old photographs appertaining to the period of your book, I must congratulate you!"

It suddenly dawned on me, after John Gaskell's departure, that I still had the task of finding a publisher for my brain child. On a near skeleton, the News, had at least, decided to put flesh on its bones. Going through the literary pages of the "Listener" I spotted an advertisement: "Authors' manuscripts required, with a view to publication. Reasonable rates. Established in 1886. Write: Arthur Stockwell, Elms Court, Ilfracombe, Devon."

"Reasonable rates", I thought, sounded good! So I despatched a copy of "Pimbo", with my writing credentials to Mr Stockwell, in the hope, that at last, publication of my work might come off!

In the meantime, I scrutinised thoroughly the Writers' Ring's view on a Stockwell's type of publishing methods, also, thinking about my dear old milk-rounds customer, with 1,500 copies stacked away in her bedroom. It seemed that in the shark infested writing world, both, vanity authors, and vanity publishers existed.

Taking Vanity publishers first, they could be viewed from two angles, one: that should an author's work be absolute rubbish, they merely act as printers. They would print and produce a book make some effort at promoting it, and the author would pay. To see his work in print, he would be well satisfied, give a few copies to close relatives, then bask in the glory of authorship, a veritable vanity author! In this case, the amount printed, would be around the 200 mark, mainly because there would be no call for further copies, the publisher, would have charged for, perhaps, 2,000 copies, and thus profit on having to print less.

From another angle, the so called Vanity publisher, would publish in his contract, the clause, that, a first novel is a very dicey affair. Money on investment in such a project would be a doubtful venture; therefore, the cash the author has to pay for his book's production, would be a kind of insurance for the publisher, should the book fail.

An initial amount of books actually printed varied from 200 to 400, but, the better type of Vanity Publisher would promise to print as many more that demand justified. Also, he would quote a reduced unit cost for the book, should the author want to take over sales himself. Royalties of course would be paid on normal circumstances, but on the author taking over sales, there would be no royalties paid.

The Vanity publisher would arrange all the usual placings, Stockwell would be responsible for book-reviews, library sales, overseas sales, copyright procedures, and the placing of a copy of the book in the Universities stipulated by the traditional publication statutes.

The money payment would be done by instalment, i.e. £400 on the acceptance of the manuscript. With the first galley proofs received by the author, another £400. On receipt of the initial copy of the work, the remainder would be paid, a sum, usually in the region of £1,500 paid.

Then, what was all the fuss about? Why do Vanity publishers come under such harsh treatment?

The main reason is, that, usually, the work they produce, literary wise, is sub-standard. Reviewers have little time for the Vanity publisher. Also booksellers rarely take on their books, making it very difficult for sales to accrue.

They, in many cases are accused of doing very little towards the promotion of the book, the advertising of *its* publication date, and getting the book into the booksellers store. The author of the book, would receive twelve copies on a complimentary basis. Some critics, pointing out the initial outlay of, say £1,500, merely was a price he paid for the ownership of just twelve volumes, a very costly affair, indeed!

On the other hand, the author, *can* make a deal with an *established* publisher. The writer, is made responsible for getting the book printed, and the publisher will store and distribute the stock as if it was one of his own titles. The publisher's handling charge being about 25% of the booksellers discount, normally 35%.

With a book selling at £5, this would leave £3.25, of this, the publisher would take £1.65, leaving £1.60 for the author. It is pretty obvious that the unit cost for printing the book, must be reasonably below £1.60, in order to give the author any kind of profit. The publisher, with his own titles, works on a multiple of five times the unit cost! Another method, is for the author to do everything himself, printing, production, taking copies around the shops, arranging the mail order sales, and arranging publicity and promotion – but for any hope of success, the author has to have a very extensive knowledge of his market.

With my head reeling from taking in so much data, I received a reply from Mr Stockwell! He thought "Pimbo" had a good chance of success, was willing to take on the project, and enclosed an official looking document for me to peruse and sign!

The document was in keeping with most I'd read concerning an author paying for his brain child to get into print. A warning about a first novel's vulnerability was given, Royalties, and promotions, were given good airing, as was the printing costs for ordinary work. Actually, there was nothing new on what I'd already read up, the cost, of producing four-hundred volumes, with a rider, that, should demand justify more copies to be printed, the publisher would do just that, was, well over a thousand pounds, to be paid by usual instalments. The book would be ready within six-months! On the day Stockwell's document arrived, the Cambridge Evening News printed the first instalment of "Pimbo". It took up two centre pages, with a picture from the archives of the Cambridgeshire Old Times Library, depicting the theme of the excerpt. A portrait of myself was also presented. I purchased four copies, one each to my children, and a spare copy for Jenny and me.

It was a great moment, as Jenny put it, "A reward for all the hard work you've put in!"

Christine and Keith, as a family unit, were present at our discussion, as to whether or not, I should chance my arm at paying out such a large sum of money for the book's publication. I pointed out immediately, that the serialisation in the local paper, should greatly enhance its sales in the bookshops, thus assuring me of getting back my initial outlay.

My children, weren't quite so sure about it. Maybe, it had only a local value, after a flurry of initial sales, might it not become moribund, and stay on the shelves?

Jenny, was all for going ahead. It was a large slice out of our savings, but, somehow, she felt it would succeed, and I would go on to write more books. With two against two, as the author, I took on myself as the casting voter, especially as Jenny too, was on my side. Laughing at my unfair casting vote role, Keith and Christine, good naturedly accepted the verdict, wishing me all the best.

That evening I phoned the News to say that Stockwell was to publish the book in the early spring.

During all of this, I experienced some interesting happenings in another field of writing, that of the article! Gathering all my nursing experiences on the psychiatric wards, into that of an article for the Nursing Mirror, which, was, to my delight, duly accepted, and paid for. I received a letter from America, it was from the Psychology Department at Smith University, Washington, D.C. It addressed me as; Dear Dr Unwin, going on to say how much they had enjoyed my article, could I forward them a copy of the Nursing Mirror, and they would be more than delighted, if I could send them more of my work.

To this I replied, signing myself off, as staff-nurse F. T. Unwin, and pointing out their error of assuming that I was a Doctor. From that moment, I received no more correspondence from them. Another case, I mischievously thought, "of leaving my cycle leaning against their office window".

Around the time of the second instalment of "Pimbo" being printed in the News, I received a phone call from John Gaskell. He asked me if I knew of a certain person in Fulbourn Hospital, it seemed that seeing the name of Stockwell as my publisher, on the note that the book would be out in the Spring, he was rather worried that I had fallen into the hands of a Vanity Publisher.

In quite honest vein, I told John all about the contact with Stockwell, that I was quite aware of the consequences, but was satisfied with the clauses in his document, adding, that I appreciated the concern of my friend at Fulbourn Hospital, and also John's concern.

A few days later, John phoned again, stating that he was doing a thesis on Vanity publishers, would I allow him to have all the documentation from Stockwell, including my contract with him. I had found John a good open lad, he had helped me a lot concerning the serialisation of "Pimbo" and although I didn't really consider myself a vanity author, I complied with his request.

In the evening, I looked up all the material I had on "the Vanity author". In the first place, self publishing, in contrast to vanity publishing, is a commercial operation aimed at making a profit for the author. I read also, that many books in the past have been produced by well-to-do spinsters, who, were quite happy to pay for their books to be published. Quite a number of now established authors, began their careers by subsidising the cost of printing. Also, with the book trade in its present doldrums, it is *not* uncommon for respectable publishers, to ask a subsidy to cover rising printing costs from their clients!

At the same time, I understood John Gaskell's motivation. He was a young man with a journalistic career to pursue, anxious, no doubt, to uncover nefarious activities in the book world. Then too, I had no cause to be smug, I was coughing up a large sum, for all I knew, I could end up in similar vein to that of the poetess, with her 1,500 unsold books? Once again I laid back awaiting for events to unfold.

Jenny, astute as ever, wasn't too happy with events. She suggested that I might be setting myself up as a guinea-pig. "A right 'nana you'll look in the eyes of the public. Vanity author! You'll have a job to live it down. They'll know all your business at the News, if as many read it as they did "Pimbo", well, then it'll take *another* year to sort it out!"

By her smile, I knew she didn't mean it, just my Jenny being a little cynical!

Even so, I consoled myself with the fact, that vanity author or not, the News had deemed "Pimbo" good enough to serialise. They had come up trumps with me, John Alexander, Rodney Tibbs had, no doubt, put in a word for me!

My week of surprises wasn't quite finished! Sitting in the Clubroom of the Manor Park camp at Hunstanton, I was confronted by an old school friend I hadn't seen for years. "You're the one that wrote "Pimbo", aren't you?" At my reply, he went on, "Funny, the Editor called me in special. Wanted to know if I knew you, what sort of chap you were, and all that. I'm the compositor foreman, you know, I told them how I was at school with you!"

Being in a mischievious mood, knowing that being illegitimate and moving from one home to another, not many people knew my real name, or my father's – I couldn't resist it! "You knew my dad then, I'll bet you don't know his name, where he lived, and what he did for a living?"

The old "school chum" blinked at me vacantly. "Can't say as I do, I only knew you at school!" came the reply.

I never troubled to find out, whether, or not, the News Editor had really called him into his office to brain wash him on my behalf. Should he have done so, I now know, why, some papers have to throw back a little of their profits, on libel-suits! Why didn't the Editor ask ME?

CHAPTER 5

Trouble Ahead

Several excerpts of "Pimbo" appeared in the News, up to the day I received notification from Stockwell as to the approaching date of the book's publication. On the eve of the great day, I received a parcel of books from Stockwell to be delivered to Bowes and Bowes, the Trinity Street bookseller. The publisher explained, that although an order form for "Pimbo" had been sent to the store, he'd received no reply, consequently it was on the cards that there would be none in stock on the day of publication. Bowes and Bowes received the books, pointing out that the order form had arrived too late for placing an order.

On the same day, I had a phone message from John Alexander to see him at the News office. He got straight down to business, telling me that John Gaskell had gathered a good deal of adverse material concerning Stockwell. To protect future writers from being conned into paying out huge sums, for little reward for their money, they intended, on the morrow to print a whole page about his activities. He wanted my permission to give the go-ahead!

Although John Gaskell had warned me of the impending article, it came as a complete surprise that it would be launched on the public, on the very day, of my book's publication. Also, as I had studied a good deal about Stockwell's kind of publishing, at least, the end result *was* getting my book into print, something that I, at one time, never thought would happen. In many ways, rightly, or wrongly, I thought publishers like Stockwell, *were* supplying a need!

I looked at John Alexander, in surprise. My mind went over a clause in the contract, stating, that first-novels were risky, therefore, the publisher was insuring himself against loss. "But, it was *me* who signed the contract, it *was* pointed out to me the reason concerned. Really, John, I have only myself to blame. I don't really feel like ratting on him!"

The News boss stared back at me. "Mr Unwin, you're a very fair man. What about the others, though, that's the reason we're running this campaign, people aren't all like you, you've shown enough talent to get your stuff on our pages, you're lucky, others will never see their name in print, unless they pay a heavy price, don't you think of them?"

I thought back on the poetess again, "I got it off my chest, I was happy to get my name in print" she'd said.

John was studying my doubting attitude. "O.K.!" he said snappily, "We'll take you down to Heffer's bookshop, we'll have you photographed behind your new book, it'll show that we aren't stopping your progress – what about it?"

It was then, my weakness of character came out. The dangling bait was something that every budding author would give his right arm for. My dreams, before actually putting pen to paper, had centred on Heffer's shop window. I'm afraid the egotistical side of me came to the fore. After all, if it were not for the old ego, not many books would ever get written!

"O.K.!" I said, "but I'm not too happy about it!"

John immediately phoned through to his transport section, and in no time, I was being whisked down to the Heffer's bookstore in Trinity Street, with a photographer beside me. Several times on the way, I had second thoughts, I almost stopped the car to get out, but, the old ego rose above it all. I'd bitten at the bait, and was being hauled in!

The store manager, hustled and bustled about, he arranged the books this way, and that way, on the large counters facing the entrance. Stockwell had sent down a cardboard replica of me, with the caption "Local author's new book". Customers were staring at me, just as though I was a Grahame Greene, or a Harold Robbins. After several changes in position and posture, the camera clicked. In the middle of this, I heard a lady ask for a copy of "Pimbo" and it made me feel good.

Later, in the evening came the hangover!!

In the centre pages of the News, was a large picture of myself, as taken in Heffer's book-store. Surrounding the picture, was the fruition of John Gaskell's work done on Stockwell. The article was splattered with Vanity Authors, Vanity Publishers, the short cuts taken by Vanity Authors in order to get into print. Not for them the hard grinding labour of trying out dozens of established publishers – they were willing to pay for "instant success". To be fair, John had not actually labelled me as a Vanity Author, but, I feel, that it was such a good imitation – that one couldn't tell the difference. Especially, in one paragraph he had mentioned the twelve complimentary copies sent to me by Stockwell, divided the twelve into the cost of my venture, and came up with the fact, that I'd paid over £120 per volume. Perhaps, not meaning to, but conveying to the reader, that all I would be getting for my money, were twelve books!

I felt it a bitter blow, especially on the very day of "Pimbo's" publication. It seemed that John, to get at Stockwell, had knocked me down as well! The fact that my writing had been good enough to receive space in the News, was completely nullified to the ordinary reader, under the clouds of the Vanity Authors and Vanity Publishers expositions!

Later in the evening, Keith and Christine came to see us, as a form of condolence. I felt a little ashamed as they viewed the article, in fact, I had a tear in my eye, when I said to Christine, "That's me finished, people won't buy books from a so-called Vanity Author!"

This remark, sprung Keith into action. "Look here, dad, that's all nonsense! I've followed John Gaskell's articles, he's a good man, trying to protect the naive. But, in one report, he'd phoned most of the book shops in the centre of the City, they came up with the fact that an established author, unless it's a very special book, doesn't expect to sell any more than four hundred copies of his book – in fact that's the average figure of most book sales! Stockwell, Vanity publisher, or not, can't do much less than that, surely?"

Jenny smiled, "Stockwell's produced a nice looking book, a cover that's attractive, a reasonable price at £2.95. He tells you in the contract, that after the first 2,000 books have been sold, you can order as many copies as you wish for a unit cost of £1. Now should you sell another 1,000 copies, the unit cost goes down even further – the whole crux of the matter is, will the book sell?"

Christine chipped in, "It seems dad, that whether, or not, the News is right, or Stockwell, writing books, for both author and publisher, in these days of money shortage, is a dicy venture. I've read of publishers going to the wall, is it because of their taking on books that don't sell, putting money into poor returns. Stockwell has been going since the 1880s, he's still going strong, he warned you about this in his contract. As far as I can see, we must sit back and hope that sales are good, if not, we must think up some method of making them good!"

Late that evening, I strolled round to Heffer's bookshop. My books, complete with cardboard replica, could be seen in the window. It seemed that Stockwell, had deposited fifty books with the store, the whole batch had been placed in the window. I counted forty-five remaining copies, which meant, that including the one the lady had bought during the photographing session, only four had been sold. As the next day was Saturday,

I expected, perhaps more sales than achieved so far.

On Sunday morning, in expectant mood, I counted them again – just another four books had left the window, in two days, only eight books had been sold.

After a week or so, the books were taken from the window, and placed on the counter. I could still see them, and was able to count them. Alas, about fifteen copies, was the resulting sale, in almost two weeks.

As a bonus, I received two letters from readers of “Pimbo”, telling of their pleasure received, and congratulating me on the work. John Gaskell, was putting the finishing touches to his articles on Stockwell. A picture of the entrance to Stockwell’s printing establishment, showed just a name posted up on the gate-post – “Stockwell Ltd – Publisher”. Either, a telephone interview, or a personal one with Stockwell was given space. The publisher reiterated much that I’ve already pointed out, also agreeing with John, that so far, he’d never had a best-selling author as a client.

Apparently, John had put together a poem of very doubtful quality, seemingly, words typed at random with little or no connection, this, he sent along to Stockwell. The publisher had replied that he could produce a booklet of further poems from John, but had little confidence in their making the grade, which would place him in the position of merely printing work from a client, which, in fact most printers would do!

He also added, that modern poetry was of such an eccentric idiom, that it was difficult at times to recognise poetry at all, which, of course, covered the arts section, bearing in mind, that a student had just won an Arts Council award, by sweeping a few leaves together, and placing them on a base of ply-wood, accompanied by a few twigs!

In being very fair, John, added a little irony to the whole affair, by admitting, that the News, during the week, had printed an advertisement from Stockwell, similar to the one that had attracted my attention in the first place!

Such was life, I thought. From that moment, I made up my mind, then come hail, rain, snow or blow, I would vindicate myself, and Stockwell, by selling Pimbo, to such an extent, that I would use up every clause in the contract, making sure that I would get back every penny spent, and enough left over to have another title printed, *and* published, by Stockwell.

At the same time, I bore no malice to John Gaskell, or the News. Newspapers, love to sensationalise, I had given them a good story, in fact, John won a literary award for his effort. I was aware too, that, maybe, some unlucky would-be-author had been conned by a Vanity Publisher, but Stockwell's contract was there for all clients to see – some fools never read the small print, and, as I had fairly pointed out to John Alexander – I'd gone into it with my eyes wide open.

Next day, I approached the manager of the W H Smith newsagency in Market Hill. I asked him, if he would care to take half-a-dozen "Pimbos" from me, as I had a few left of my complimentary copies. Rather reluctantly, he accepted the offer. On fetching my newspaper from the shop on the following morning, (I lived just two hundred yards away) I noticed that he'd placed them as far back on his book-shelf as possible, almost needing a blood-hound to find them.

Each ensuing day, I checked on how many copies had been sold, after a week's check-out, I found just one copy had gone. Arriving back at my flat I told Jenny of my discovery, adding "I reckon in a few hours I could sell those books down any old street!" Jenny's reply was to have an outstanding effect on my career as an author.

"Well, why don't you, it's no good talking about it – do it!"

I had not *really* meant what I had said, but her reply was the equivalent of my being struck on the head with a hammer. Many things get said, just for the sake of talking – but this time, I was to put my feet where my mouth was!

Being a psychiatric nurse, meant a good deal of shift work, I had a day off each week, with an occasional week-end. Also, my times on duty were fixed, either 7 a.m. – 2 p.m. or 2.15 p.m. – 9 p.m., giving my flexible times in which to do my selling. Some years back I had been a brush salesman, this had given me a good background in door-to-door selling. I had been head-salesman of my district for several years, and had won many cups and trophies. A vital factor in selling technique, was to give yourself a quota! – then stick to it, never come home unless you have made your quota!

My first problem was to choose a territory. True to my silly weak nature, I decided that for the sake of the shops storing my book, I would not

Counting the books for sale in Heffers window

work, in the City. Also, I felt I did not want to rely on sympathy sales. I wanted to sell the book, purely on its merit – so, I chose Bedford, of all places, to sell a book about a boy's childhood in Cambridge. I felt, that if I could sell a book there, I could sell it anywhere!

Purchasing a shopping trolley, in which to place my books, on a certain Saturday morning, with my whole family present, I left with their best wishes ringing in my ears. Taking twenty copies as my quota, I had timed myself to catch the 7.45 a.m. bus to Bedford.

The journey was of one hour duration, I arrived at the bus depot at a little before nine o'clock. I chose a group of residential homes on an estate just off the Goldington Road. Cuttings, from the News, (minus the Gaskell outpourings of course) I had fitted into a kind of plastic wallet, which I could display to my potential buyers. Two letters, I'd received from grateful readers, I'd managed to manipulate into a sort of prospectus. Armed with all this, I approached my territory. As I passed Goldington Church, the clock on the tower was striking nine o'clock. The return bus to Cambridge left at 6.15 p.m., giving me bags of time, I assumed to sell my quota.

Although I'd been a brush salesman for twelve years, the work being one of the hardest type of selling imaginable – I *was* nervous, as I approached my first house. Success meant a great deal to me, I didn't want to let Jenny down, or Keith and Christine, who had both come specially to see me off. Pride, is a very hard task-master, and I certainly felt under its whip.

The first person I found in, was a rather elderly lady. I did my little party-piece, at the end of which, she said, "If it had been about Bedford, I'd have one. Spent my childhood in Bedford, St Leonard's Street, do you know it? No, sorry mister, it looks a nice book, but I don't like Cambridge, anyway!"

I went on and on, from one street to another, quite a few people were out. At some homes, I got a cold reception, "Never buy at the door, my old mum told me that, the day I got married – ain't that right, Bert?" She shouts through the hall, at her spouse in the kitchen. Without waiting for Bert's reply I moved onto the next house.

There were one, or two, near misses. One person had only a twenty pound note, another gentleman would have bought, but his wife had gone out shopping and taken all the money!

On, and on, I walked, with my selling experience bolstering me up against the constant "No – thank yous". House after house, flat after flat, bungalow after bungalow, old men, young men, housewives, widows, widowers, pensioners, newly weds, shacker ups, and a pot pourri of cosmopolitans. Looking at my watch I saw it was twelve o'clock, in three hours, I'd sold nothing! I just couldn't return to Cambridge empty handed. After the 6.15 bus, the last one would be 8.45 p.m., well then, I'd walk, and walk, until I caught the last bus home, should I miss that, I'd cadge a lift home, but I certainly wasn't going back until I'd sold my quota of twenty "Pimbos".

Now, the one thing that a good salesman learns, is that the law of average is on his side. It's scientifically impossibe, for one, to knock, door, after door, for hour upon hour, without making a sale. I'd learned this the hard way, I once had gone five hours brushselling without a sale, and *then* reached my quota.

Another thing in my favour, was the dinner time factor. From twelve noon until 2 p.m., more people are likely to be at home, than the hours from 9 a.m. onwards. Also, more members of the family are likely to be present during the meal break, thus making the likelihood of a sale more on the cards.

My break came around twelve-thirty. A lady, who came to the door, had a father living in Cheddar's Lane, Cambridge. Luckily, I knew him, in fact, had gone to school with him. She shouted excitedly to someone at the back of the house, who, turned out to be a friend from Cambridge. They both purchased a book, which, had indeed, more than broken my duck.

My wanderings had taken me onto the Putnoe estate, a new housing estate, having a large amount of youngsters from seven years upwards. I pushed the fact that "Pimbo" would make a good Christmas present, thus, increasing my sales to ten. With ten more sales to make, I set out again with renewed vigour.

However, it turned out to be far from plain sailing! A group of houses, different from most, seemed to house housewives with a great reliance on their husbands. At each call, the wife would shout out the name of her spouse, then retreat back into the kitchen. I found the husband, to be of great muscular development, who, stood feet astride, arms akimbo, and with a fixed stare, greeted me with, "Well, what's it then?" After calling at three homes, I found the answer, when I spotted a police helmet hanging in the hall, they were police houses.

Having the last laugh on a rather haughty wife, gave me great satisfaction. At one time, I had played cricket for the Cambridge Police, with Bedford Police being our opponents. The copper coming to the door, recognised me, called me in, and over a cup of tea, we talked about our various matches. The wife, rather reluctantly served tea, with my having the cheek to ask for another cup! At the end of our conflab, he bought a couple of books.

At another house, as I looked through the front window, I didn't like the look of an elderly gentlemen slumped in a chair. My nursing experience told me that something was wrong. The lady coming to the door, seemed unaware of her lodger's predicament. On my bringing her attention to him, it was found that he'd taken an overdose of tablets, with the empty bottle at his side.

As I finished off my sales further along the street, I heard the siren, as the ambulance dashed to the house. It was striking three o'clock, as I sold my last "Pimbo". I was able to catch an earlier bus than expected, musing on the journey home, that things had turned out well!

Jenny would be more than pleased, and I had signed my autograph twenty times, something I thought would never happen to me!

CHAPTER 6

The Best Seller That Never Was!

After my Bedford success, Jenny, and I, were going over the requirements needed for me to break even with my book future. Selling twenty each day, should I be able to manage a five day stint, would mean, one hundred books. It would therefore, take ten weeks in order to get rid of a thousand volumes.

True to John Gaskell's survey on books sold by established writers, "Pimbo" had sold four-hundred copies. A majority of these, no doubt were publication-day sales, which, usually result in a flurry of sales, then, for the book to become moribund on the shelves. Mr Stockwell had kept me up to date with his sales. Thirty or so in the various libraries spread over the country. Shop sales showed the book stores usually took in no more than from 1 – 6. Library distributors ordered twenty or so, so it was plain to see that the bulk of sales would have to be sold by myself. Royalties, in my case, due, to the small amount of sales from sources other than myself, would not amount to very much, and Stockwell would be justified in making those payments to me on an annual basis, as did most publishers.

In between door-to-door selling, I managed to get an article accepted in the "Good Health" magazine, I had written about my experiences on the drug addiction ward at Fulbourn Hospital – as a nurse of course!

The Cambridge Evening News, did me proud, by printing a nice report on my door-to-door selling, sending out a photographer with me as I did my rounds. One morning, during my duty at the hospital, I was now a charge-nurse, the telephone rang! To my utter surprise, it was from the B.B.C., the Anglia T.V. station wanted to do a programme, I could hardly believe my luck!

David Cass, with his permanent crew, came down to the Hospital to arrange a programme, during which, I would do my selling stint at the door. We chose an estate at Cherry Hinton, arriving at 10 a.m. It was a bad time, most of the women, having taken their kiddies to school, would be at work. Rather embarrassingly, I strolled from door-to-door, hoping very soon to give the camera crew something to do. At last we hit on a nice lady, whose husband I knew quite well as a local gas fitter. A chat at the door, with the lady holding her small child in her arms, as the cameras clicked, made, I felt, a good start.

Amazingly, the next call was made at the daughter, whose mother had lived a few doors from my house in Keynes Road, a Mrs Rumbelow. David Cass, a true professional, made the most of this encounter, then taking me in front of a group of newly built houses, with everything set up for an out-door interview, he quizzed me on my unusual break into the literary world. Somehow, I didn't feel nervous, in many respects, I must have felt like anyone, who, after a good deal of ups-and-downs, had finally got a few breaks.

A plane, from the nearby Marshall's aerodrome, kept passing over-head, stopping and starting our interview. David looked up and said good humouredly, "Must be the folk from the other Channel, trying to put a spanner in our work!"

Although not unduly nervous, I kept saying "How'm I doing, not making a mess of it, am I?"

After the final take Mr Cass, looking at his watch, pointed out there was plenty of time for the film to be put on the 2 o'clock train to Norwich, for the edition on the 6 o'clock programme. He suggested, that we had a break, while one of his crew would take the film down to the station.

It was a lovely day, we sat on the grass verge of a field overlooking Fulbourn Hospital. I told him of my plan to write a book about my nursing experiences.

David, told me of his great interest in sport, of his daughter, who was a Junior Tennis Champion, to my surprise, he spoke of his desire to become a sports-presenter (he accomplished, just that, a few years later). David asked me if I liked poetry, on my reply, he suggested that I do a little spot for him to finish the day's work.

Once again, the T.V. equipment was set up, and I did my piece. I wasn't really happy about it, I read it out, with my rather heavy glasses propped on the end of my nose. The poem, which, luckily, or not, I had with me, was rather a sad poem, about the life of a patient at Fulbourn.

David, charitable as ever, said it was lovely (but it was never shown on the edited version of our filming) maybe, he'd forgotten to put in the film? Eventually the day of my little bit of heaven came to its end.

In the evening, Jenny, and I, sat awaiting the great event of my television debut. My bald patch was very evident, my voice sounded raspy, and not at all attractive. They say that no-one is ever satisfied with his voice on telly. All in all, I felt that I hadn't done *too* badly. The little cameo, including the gas fitter's wife, was not put in, but Mrs Rumbelow's daughter, came out well, talking to me at the door.

Next day, with all the hullaboo of the television experiences over, Jenny and I got down to serious talk concerning my writing career. The doubts, shame, and publicity of the Vanity Author shindig had been buried for good. I had sent Stockwell all the News articles concerning him, and told the publisher that I had decided to take on bookselling myself, this meant that I required two thousand books of "Pimbo", run off, at a unit cost to me of £1, in accordance with the contract I had signed. From the moment Stockwell agreed, the boundary of Vanity Publisher, and Vanity Author, had passed over into the bounds of a *commercial* publishing and bookselling contract – which, in the first place I fully expected it to be! The book, was priced at £2.95, but, at the door I sold it for £2. This price enabled me to cover the cost of bus fares, and eating out facilities, when a long day kept me from home. Shoe leather of course, although a seemingly laughing matter, came into the reckoning. I had worked out, the average sale of my door-to-door project, was, *one* call in ten. This meant that to sell ten books, I had to call on one hundred people. This does not account for the amount of people *not* at home. I reckoned that four people out of ten are out. This of course means that the one in ten average takes in only people who *are* in! Give or take a bad day, or good day, accounting for "outs", to sell my quota of twenty books, I had to call on 240 people.

Many houses have long drives, some have steps to the door which can be very tiring. A fair amount of time in selling discourse is taken up, which means that visiting 240 homes can be an exhausting business. Although a customer may readily buy a book, the gap between the knock at the door, and the moment the client arrives at the door, is unconsciously to the best of salesmen, a fairly tense moment, especially if sales had not been too satisfactory. Multiply this by 240, then you are eating up a lot of nervous energy.

There is no room for rudeness "I never buy at the door!" "Come back when, my husband is at home", "I'm sorry, I've not time to stand at the door!" has to be taken with a smile, the salesman cannot afford to leave the house under a cloud, he will be coming back again with his new product.

As the days and months went by the sale of "Pimbo" went on. I was now sixty years of age, and could take retirement at the hospital. Jenny had been suffering with rheumatoid-arthritis, a very painful malady with a progressive diagnosis – so, as I was expected at times to do night shifts, I felt, that taking on writing as a full time job would ensure my being at home with Jenny. Thus, it was, that I retired, although the hospital told me "I could come back, whenever I wished, and for as long as I wanted to!"

Now and again, I would take stock of myself. At sixty, with a book proving successful, and, against all odds; after selling enough books to cover my initial outlay, I *could* call it a day. I'd read in many boxing articles that the reason why a lot of present day boxers fail, is because they are no longer "hungry fighters" as were their predecessors. Also, there *was* such a thing as a writing-bug, a tough little fellow, always under your skin, biting away at your inner-resolve, like a barnacle never letting go. Watching Frank Delaney on a T.V. programme, made me even more determined to go on. The programme was about Vanity Authors, and their publishers. In the sum up, Frank put forward, "I think the reason why some writers' have to resort to Vanity Publishing is because their work just isn't good enough!"

This stung me into action. No doubt, in some respects he was right. Tucked away, amidst the little housing estates, was someone, with perhaps, two hundred unsold volumes stashed away – but, still looking lovingly at their brain child. I was thinking of "Watership Down", "Life of the Jackal", "Fanny Hill", and many, many other best-sellers, that had had a very rough passage, and, were, if not for their creators assuming the roles of hungry-fighters, would never have seen the light of day.

Also, in another field, we have the "Opportunity Knocks" programme, which, has produced a galaxy of stars over the years, stars, who may never have seen the foot lights from behind, but, for someone giving the unseeded amateurs a chance.

Maybe in authorship, the opportunity doesn't knock often enough, as Jesus pleads "Behold, I stand at the door and knock – will *you* let me in?"

Indeed, I had become a hungry-fighter!

"Pimbo" had now sold 3,000 copies, the majority from my door-to-door sales. According to Stockwell's latest data, in which he docketed every sale, and its destination, 250 books had been sold, including the bookshop sales at 400 copies, this produced a figure of 650, well short of a thousand copies. However, book-shops were still sending into me requests for further copies, which meant there was no ceiling as to the amount that might be sold (actually, to date, "Pimbo" has been into the homes of 15,000 people).

Finishing "Dew on my Feet", I was able, now, to use Stockwell in the role of printer. The money from Pimbo sales, would cover the cost of printing and production. My new book told of my experience as a psychiatric nurse. The public were a little afraid of anything connected with the mind. They would think nothing of going into hospital for the repair of any other part of their bodies, but to the mind, a strong taboo! In the book, I used no technical jargon at all, just bringing out what went on between patient and nurse, on the strength, that a mother, washing, feeding, dressing and cuddling her child, would have a life advantage in "knowing" her own child, than that of a teacher, social worker, or, even the doctor.

Extreme cases of course were an exception.

To ascertain there would be no back lash on my work, a copy of the manuscript was shown to Dr Clark, the then Medical Superintendant. His reaction, "You write splendidly, I found the book most fascinating!"

Being the author of "Pimbo", amounted to several requests for my attending women's meetings, schools, and other groups. Among the first, was Miss Margaret Cox, the Headmistress of the Brunswick School, a school which had been mentioned in the book. I enjoyed very much the visit to the school; at the time they were using "Pimbo" for lessons on sociology. I was struck by the brightness of the class-rooms, the colourful projects pinned up on the wall. The sharpness, and happy looks of the pupils. But, above all, the way they were dressed took my eye!

Not for them the plimsols of the thirties, a sixpenny touch at Woolly's. In lieu of drab Jerseys for the boys were snappy shirts, or brightly coloured T-shirts, with smartly creased trousers, and belts, supported by sturdy shoes, in place of the steel-capped heavy boots from the Police station. The girls, in their pretty dresses, bright cardigans, and stylish, almost womanish shoes. They carried Addidas holdalls to school, or B.O.A.C. satchels, and they had a set of clothes and equipment for each sport in which they indulged.

Now, I realised that to do this, Mums had to have credit vouchers, work at two jobs, maybe, the whole set up could lead to an economic explosion. But, by Jiminy, it *was* there, no child need to be embarrassed on the way to school, no radiators required to dry out cardboard-sole shoes, and it showed in their faces, bright, confident kids, who, swam, played hockey, netball, even chess, visited museums had their photos in the News on Speech Day, formed a school choir, where they sang with gusto "England's Green and Pleasant Land," and above all had been introduced by Miss Cox to the beauty of real music!

They sat wide-eyed, poles apart from that which I was to talk to them about.

Speaking at W.I.s was great fun at times. Attending one hall, which the Institute rented, at the beginning, the lady chairman wasn't aware that I charged nothing for my little talks, my relying simply on selling a few books at the close of the meeting. Forthcoming schedules were read out by forthright buxom ladies. Result of last week's raffle, and little get well messages for those not present. The Chairlady with eyes meeting my gaze every few moments – dropped her ace!

"I'm afraid, ladies, I have bad news for you! It's quite possible that, as the rent for the hall has increased out of all proportion our use of the hall is under profound jeopardy – by next year, we may have to look out for a new venue!"

Before starting my talk, I put her at ease, by telling her that my talk was free. It brought a new radiance to her face, but, it made me realise, that a lot of hard work and sacrifices go on behind the jumble-sales, sales of work, and harvest suppers.

At another talk, I was nattering away about the poverty stricken days of my childhood. I used to place bricks on the road, so that coal laden carts on their way to the Gas works, would be made to sway, as they ran over the bricks, thus, allowing lumps of coal from the heavily laden carts, to fall on to the road. With an old tin bucket, I used to collect the "black diamonds", and run home, with the thoughts of a roaring fire to enjoy – a very rare treat in those days!

My eye caught the set features of a woman sitting in the front row, she was glaring at me daggers.

A little intermission ensued, after which question time would embrace the remainder of the evening. I asked her what was wrong?

"You should be ashamed of yourself, you were actually stealing coal!"

Thinking of the poor times in those days where, often it was candles for the only light in the house, and we couldn't afford coal, I couldn't resist saying "I think Jesus would have forgiven a small boy for taking a little warmth into his house!" I suppose the old adage that it "takes all sorts to make a world" held good in the woman's ideals. I found out later, that the lady was a spinster, who did good work in the church – but, never having had children, she stuck rigidly by the letter to her doctrines, and, as I'm afraid, we are all guilty at times, of leaving out the Spirit.

Amazingly, some weeks later, I knocked at a door, and, who should answer, but, the dear lady. She purchased a book, called me in, and apologised for her little "Do" at the meeting, over a cup of tea, all was made well! "Pimbo" had now reached sales of over 4,000. When taking in reorders to the shops, I found the shop personnel very friendly, and I often had chats with Mr Gibbs the departmental manager. He told me of books, that never made the grade, they lay dormant for weeks, finally to become remaindered.

Door to door in Bedford

He told me of a dear lady authoress with a book on family history, (a little pricey, he thought) she would come into the book department, ferret out her particular brain child from the shelves, then place it in a more prominent position. Mr Gibbs had seen many books remaindered, and, pointed out that the literary world could be very cruel at times. "Hyping" nowadays was the "in" thing. Books, were hyped into best-sellers before they were actually written. He told me of one such book, which literary agents and publishers had gone over the top with. The publisher had paid the "author" thousands of pounds in advance-fees, photographs of him, living it up on the Spanish holiday resorts were seen in the national press.

When the book was finally published, and on the shelves, sales were almost minimal. A leading book store was so puzzled that they sent an expert down to investigate. His report, "There was no punctuation. No continuity of thought, or theme. No story line, at all, characterisation minus, plus, the book was a pathetic jumble of words!"

Mr Gibbs smiled. "It puzzled me, so I read further into the story of the book. It seemed that an overworked literary agent had read the manuscript, late one evening. He phoned his publisher, who, at the time was in bed. The great man, without having read the manuscript, put into motion, wheels, that hyped the book onto its present ridiculous state, even obtaining film rights!

"But why?" I asked.

Mr Gibbs made it plain. Sheer greed. Some publishers were desperate to find best sellers, they were afraid that a rival might get in first. At times, publishers turn down books which turn out to be best sellers, "Watership Down" was just one of many. A million pounds could be won, or lost, on as fickle decision. In the case of the "Best Seller, that never was!" (a title given to the article, by a renowned literary journal) the publisher, perhaps relying on his agents integrity, took a chance on the basis of "some you win, some you lose!" without actually reading the manuscript.

I was learning fast! Selling my one-hundred-and-twenty books a week, was a hard grind. (I was now managing a six-day week) It kept me out of the super class, but, I was meeting people. I had made up my mind to keep on writing, with an ambition of writing at least a dozen books. I would write about all the old characters I knew in Cambridge, both rich and poor, sick or strong. Mothers, who had brought up families of eight, in houses one-up, one-down, the children turning into good honest people, the back-bone of the working force in Cambridge.

Not much kudos for mum! But she'd get her name in my book.

"Dew on my Feet" was now out. "Pimbo" sales were covering its printing costs. It received a good review in the News and the Nursing Mirror. "A book that should make every young lady, leaving school, want to become a psychiatric nurse!" was the leading nursing journal's review.

I was on my way. The "way" in my case, along the path leading to the house! One day, perhaps, I might meet the publishers of the "Best-seller, that never was" – but, until then I'm quite happy.

CHAPTER 7

Knock on any Door

Things were going along nicely, I was getting letters from readers as far away as Canada, Australia, Germany, and Holland. Many with their ground roots in Cambridge, who, had picked up sticks to try a new life elsewhere. Now and again a criticism, "It wasn't number ten, Leeke Street, it was number twelve!" "My father was seventy when he died, not eighty!" Someone, went down to the News office, to say that I never had T.B. at all! Apparently, they *must* have been talking about an entirely different person. Dr Patan Phillips didn't send his child patients to Holt Sanatoriam for nothing! Remembering that I was writing about events that had taken place fifty years ago a little poetic licence has to be afforded. I smiled when I came across Clive James, he had written a story of his childhood, which, had provoked such controversy concerning petty things, which, I have mentioned, that he decided to call his sequel "Unreliable Memoirs", which, turned out to be a best-seller. Sometimes I came across a person, usually very aged, who'd say, "You didn't mention so-and-so in your book, I could write a book myself, knew 'em all I did!" It often turned out that I *had* mentioned so-and-so, the old chap hadn't read my book, and was feeling frustrated to think that someone *had* written a book. On the cover of "Pimbo", the name of a well known Rag, Bone and Metal Merchant was visible, that of George Wheatley. This well known lovable character, was the means of young scally-wags, such as myself, of earning enough money to go the pictures, through collecting rags, bottles, or anything of valuable metal, which we took to Wheatley's scrap yard in Staffordshire Street. George would pay a half-penny for a clean jam-jar, or, a penny for a pickle jar, and sixpence for a bundle of rags. One day, my being out at the time, Jenny let in a young man, who seemingly couldn't thank me enough. It had transpired, that dear old George had died, but a few months before he died, with his brain a little demented, he clutched my book in his hands, pointing out his name on the cover to all who visited him. His son, who, it was, that called on me, was so pleased to know that his old dad had gone peacefully!

Sales of "Dew of my Feet" were going reasonably well, but, I found the public a little afraid of a book relating to mental illness. The reason, I felt, was, that, many families, had *someone*, either, uncle, aunt, niece or nephew, grand parents, or even their own kin, who, at sometime or other, had occasion to enter a psychiatric hospital – it was a taboo handed down over the ages, with the "Yellow Ticket" or, over the wall, symbolic of their fears. Even so, I received a letter from a vicar in Wales, who rated "Dew on my Feet" as, on a par, with a recent best-seller on a similar subject. My sales, each day were charted on a pro-forma, giving a detailed account of every book I had sold since my Bedford visit. The amount of money received was also shown, this of course for the benefit of the tax man. From the start, with visions of a huge tax bill plopping on the mat, I had engaged the services of Spicer & Pegler, renowned chartered-accountants.

Although, I was now well over sixty, I was paying at the rate of thirty-percent, which, of course, stopped me from ever being a rich man. The run-off of "Dew on my Feet" was 5,000 copies, "Pimbo", so far had registered 5,000 sales, with sales still coming from Stockwell, and the shops. My dealings with Stockwell, as publisher, were coming to an end, in retrospect, he had turned out trumps! He was sending me books ordered, well packaged, with absolute minimum carriage charges. The unit cost gave me a chance to pay off the initial cost of "Pimbo's" production and subsidised "Dew on my Feet".

Of future books, I intended to find a local printer, and carry on writing as long as possible. Finding a 5,000 run-off quite practical, this would be my target for future titles!

One day, returning home from a long stint, I had occasion to call at the local cafe in Bradwells Court in Cambridge's new shopping precinct. Sitting at a table, whilst enjoying a cake, an elderly lady approached me. Somehow, I thought I knew her face, but, realised that seeing thousands of faces over the last year, or so, I may well have been mistaken.

"You're Mr Unwin, aren't you? The man who wrote 'Pimbo'?", armed with cup of coffee, she renewed her attack. "I would like you to write my life story, I'll pay you a thousand pounds, what do you say?"

"A £1,000 to write my story"

Studying her face, my mind went back to a large house on a private estate in Royston, a town just outside Cambridge. The lady of the house invited me in, bringing into the lounge a tray laden with a silver tea set. The house was spacious, beautifully furnished, and the owner seemed a woman of more than substantial means.

She purchased a copy of "Pimbo" and one of "Dew on my Feet". After which, she went into a long tirade against her present husband, who, it seemed, was running favourite in the infidelity stakes.

Feeling this a rather delicate subject, I tried to side-track, but the lady went on. "You must, as a writer, be well versed in matrimonial problems. I suppose you find writing quite easy, just a matter of waiting for inspiration to come, then away you go – like billy-ho!"

I smiled, this was an old chestnut. I pointed out that it was a complete myth that writing was mainly inspired. Inspiration was a common denominator, with hard work the driving force.

Through the window I could see a large car coming into the drive.

Thinking my presence might jeapardize any chance she might have of being the innocent party, I made an excuse to leave, pointing out that I had a bus to catch. My experience in the psychiatric field had insulated me against womans' wiles! There now in front of me, whom, I am sure, was the self-same woman. "Did you not, sometime ago, live in Royston?" I asked.

The woman shook her head. "No you're mistaken, I must have a double, others have told me so, yes, that's it, I must have a double!" She went on to ask again for my consent to write her autobiography.

Reasoning it all out, I refused. The work would take at least a year, during which my earning capacity would be greatly reduced. Finding a publisher, too, wouldn't be easy. It made me realise the true lot of publishers, *who*, would risk spending good money on an untried commodity!

Trying a shot in the dark, I asked her where she was now living. "I've moved recently, over at a village called Hartwell, I'm renovating three cottages into one, my husband has left me, I've no family!"

The whole affair seemed dicey. Later, I realised that I might have turned down a great story. The ingredients were there, a love triangle, intrigue, during the renovation of the cottages, what might she find behind the old fire places? While writing her story, I may well have found myself under the influence of an evil woman, willing me to write reams of suspense. Had she murdered her husband? Why did she deny ever living at Royston?

On my way home, I realised that after a tiring day, I had been over re-acting. The poor woman *may* have needed help; however, after a nice chat with Jenny, we decided that the whole thing be written off – perhaps one day I might make a story out of it! With perhaps more than my share of inspiration!

Following on the heels of the £1,000 offer for writing a lady's autobiography came another strange incident. With my taking over the selling of the books I'd written, it was my job to invoice all sales to the shops in compliance with their order. Lackadaisical payment by some publishers and indeed bookshops, was an eternal grouse by many local authors. It seemed to work on the principle of paying the big fish, the minnows would look after themselves!

A certain large bookshop owed me £184 for books supplied. I waited well over a year for payment, then put a reminder quoting the invoice number of the original invoice. Some weeks later, to my pleasure, I received a cheque for £184. The shock came a month later, when I received a cheque for a similar amount. Taking it back to their accounts department, I pointed it out to the manager the discrepancy entailed. The cheque had been duplicated. The manager, thanked me profusely, and promised to look into the matter by contacting his Head Office, from where the payments came.

Meantime, a similar amount of money was involved with the same store concerning a fresh supply of books from me. A few months later, I sent in a reminder, with a view of cutting out the long delay of the first payment. To my surprise, the invoice was returned, with a rider that the invoice was a duplicate, meaning that they intended *not* to pay for the books. Calling in to see the local manager, the matter was clarified at once with his Head Office, and I received my payment!

The amazing incident was triplicated by three other book shops, each, paying me cheques twice on one invoice. These were of course, returned with my pointing out the errors.

Now, the points I'm bringing out, are these: I send off an Invoice, say No. 20. After a long delay I send in a reminder, quoting Invoice No. 20. A cheque for the amount on Invoice 20 is sent to me. But, some weeks later, I receive a cheque for a similar amount on the Reminder invoice, quoting Invoice 20.

The fact that this error cropped up in four cases, all told, asks the questions. Is the computer to blame? How many times does this mistake occur? Could a crook, spotting this loop-hole, capitalise on the errors?

To offset this problem, three out of the four bookshops decided to eliminate the errors by; paying me monthly, or paying on receipt of the books. The odd one out, made no change, even allowing the incident to happen again. I decided to stop supplying that particular book-store.

My journeys around the houses, brought many interesting meetings with a hotch-potch of people interested in becoming writers. One particular lady, told me she had read every paper-back she could lay her hands on, concerning the art of being an author. She had covered every aspect; preparation of manuscripts, language, English grammar, style, form, and format, literary agents, and marketing. But still, she had failed to hit the jack-pot, after sending off forty short stories – there was nothing!

Looking across to me over a cup of coffee, she said "What do *you* make of it?"

It was a big question, I thought of the American Journalist, who, after analysing four published stories, juggling them around without altering their context, or quality, came up with a blank.

"Maybe, no paperback can manufacture a writer, maybe there has to be a basic talent of some element, just needing a catylistic fuse. Then again, there are so many at it! Take a short story competition in any Womans' Journal – there are thousands of entries – they can't all win!" I replied.

"But there's something else, isn't there, be honest?" she almost pleaded. I wanted to help her, I wanted to help everyone of the hundreds I had met on the doorstep, who, had asked the same question. Knowing I'd been lucky, fully aware, that, had I not allowed Stockwell to publish "Pimbo", I would be just like this lady, and thousands more. I knew that I was no better writer than all those people, it was just that I'd made my own breaks, but, I knew one thing you didn't have to be a college professor, an elite dignitary, the most people wanted, was something they could understand, without having to consult a dictionary after every sentence!

So I told her about the little music master in the T.V. series "Fame". After listening to a young student play technically faultlessly, a special piece, the music teacher had shown little response. The student blew his top, "What do you want from me – blood? I've studied this piece, practised for hours, everyone tells me I'm good, but you! I've read every technicality concerning this work – where do I go from here?"

The old master, paused, then smiled "You are correct. Technically, you play faultlessly, but you don't play *music*! Before the war, I studied as you do, I perfected my playing to such an extent, that a false note would jar me, as though a road digger, was at my elbow. Then came the war, as a German Jew I was hounded from pillar to post, moved like a rat from one underground sewer to another, almost starved, almost frozen to death, – but I survived. When I returned to my beloved violin, I began to play real music. I played with soul, I played as though I were thanking God for my deliverance. I played for dead Jews, the helpless children in the gas chambers. I played for the sheer joy of being able to play – that's why I played real music!"

The young student, smiled. "I'm, so sorry, Sir. I understand, you have taught me a great deal – I'll never be impatient again!"

My lady customer poured out another coffee. "Phew!" She gasped, "What a mouthful, but do you think, maybe my English puts me back, I'm not a good speller, would that be a reason for my rejection-slips?"

This was another question asked many times at the door. I suppose many saw in me, someone, who had actually done what they were trying to achieve. I reckon, that one in ten housewives, have, at sometime or other, set designs on becoming a writer. I told her that talent would out, editors would not worry in the least about spelling, when they're looking at a potential bestseller, anything goes! The original manuscript of "Jaws" was written on a scrap of paper. On first sight, it was almost laughed at. It was rewritten, scrapped, then rewritten again, to become a blockbuster in book and film form. But, the potential *was* there – from the start!

Then again, grammar and words, are rapidly changing. The Oxford Dictionary now accepts "It's me" as well as the more correct, but starchy "It is I!" Colloquial, Vernacular, Idiomatic phrases, all are accepted in both dialogue and characterisation, as a *natural* way of speaking. Past tenses, present tenses, and present continuous tenses, look after themselves when the author is writing about an image before him, what is actually happening at the time!

Such phrases as "This moment of time!" "Basically speaking" "I, personally speaking!" "Across the board" "Having said that – I'll" can be heard regularly on both radio, and television, spoken by educated people, and meaning absolutely nothing!

I pointed out to her, that every writer has a blind spot. This sentence was heard on "World at One". "My first object was to endeavour to ascertain what the others were going to do."

As, "Brush up your grammar", points out: "Try to find out!" would be much simpler.

"The lachrymal ducts, exudated a saline secretion, which ran like rivulets down the undulating folds of his features!" This sounds very highfaluting, but the shortest sentence in the Bible, reads: "Jesus wept." – more emphatic, I'm sure!

Feeling things were getting a little heavy, we both called it a day. The lady was very grateful, she felt that a good deal had been clarified in her mind. "The only thing, do I have to become a prisoner-of-war, to be able to write real stories?" She asked jokingly, I told her, as I told many, to join a good correspondence writing school, and take it from there!

As we got to the door she stopped and returned to the kitchen, coming out with a list of names on a memo pad. "It's my Christmas shopping list. It's just struck me, that I could use your books as presents for my grandchildren, I'll take five copies of "Pimbo", and two of "Dew on my Feet".

It was amazing how things work out! I *had* spent rather too long at her house. Getting carried away in your desire to help a fellow writer, is a good thing, as long as it doesn't curtail your selling time. On one occasion, I remember seeing a whole line of cars outside their houses in a certain street. This was a pleasant sight for the door-to-door salesman, but, after being held up by an over talkative lady at the door, as I came away, the last car was just moving off, leaving a trail of possibly empty houses!

Going home my thoughts returned to the lady with whom I'd spent a teaching session. It reminded me, how in my early days as a writer I had doubts, such as she, whether or not, *I* was a writer. I reasoned that everyone has a book inside them, possibly, two or three. Writing one's memoirs, too, wasn't such an achievement, after all, I was writing only about what I knew.

But, one day, I decided on writing a short story. I had the blank page of virgin foolscap before me, with no plot, characters, setting, or what have you? I found, that I was able to start, carry on unfolding a story, still with no real theme in mind, characters came popping in and out, as though they'd been hired by a film director.

Next day, returning to my half finished tale, I had to read over what I'd written, because I had forgotten its theme so far. To my delight I was able to carry on with story, as though I'd never left it. Everything slipped into place, and the story was finished. What's more, it sold first time out!

A few years later, reading the life story of a famous author, I found, that, he too, could fill a blank page from scratch, and often, at certain stages in his story, had no idea how it was going to end.

He worked out, that if *he* didn't know, his reader wouldn't either, thus, making it a surprise ending.

CHAPTER 8

Libel

Things were going well for me. "Pimbo", had been turned into a "Talking Book", in aid of the Blind Association. It was also being used in the Progressive Reading Schools, a new scheme to assist better reading skills for both adults and children. My plans for a third book had reached fruition, I had just completed "What Pimbo Did Next!" Finding a printing press, to print, and produce my book, was my next mountain to climb.

The Burlington Press, in Foxton, was my choice. Furthermore, their little paste-up artist, I discovered, was also very skilled in line drawings. I decided that Janet would give atmosphere to the book, so I engaged her to do just that!

During my rounds, I picked up a lot of little snippets of gossip, one, to the effect, that, sometimes, authors were liable to be sued for various kinds of libel, copyright infringements, and so forth. Another thing, I was now about to take over the role of publisher. Did I have to register? Could the registration be turned down, on the strength of my not having the capital to take on a wide spectrum of publications?

It was then I decided to join the "Society of Authors", a body I'd heard lots of goods things about. I wrote off to enquire about regulations, and what one had to do to become a member. In their reply, I found, that to become a member the rules were very stringent!

A potential member, had to have had, two full length novels, published by an established publisher, and to have received royalties on both titles. Four short stories, to be paid for by established journals, was the next stipulation. For full measure, at least two articles, again to be paid for by reputable magazines or journals.

Although I had verified those requests, I wondered whether my work would be considered good enough!

The regulations did not end there! A copy of each part of the "pass" rules, had to be sent off to the Society's Headquarters in Drayton Gardens, London. With great trepidation, I parcelled up a copy of each of my successes in the literary world, and awaited the verdict. At the same time, I enquired about my new status as a publisher, and what it entailed.

Three months later, when I'd almost given up hope, the reply came. My work had been accepted, I'd been made an Associate Member of the Society of Authors, the annual fee, as I was now a publisher, was one of a slight concession, that of £24.00.

To my relief, the question of my becoming a publisher, was, in no way, as stringent as the rules of membership. It merely states, that, should an author write a book, get it printed.

take on responsibility for its sale, well, then, he becomes a publisher.

I would say, that every author should become a member of a society such as this. It covered every aspect in a writer's world. Libel, insurance, Publishers, Literary awards, Literary meetings, all over the globe. A list of "rogue publishers" was made in their quarterly copy, and authors were invited to write in about lackadaisical royalties payments, lack of book promotion, etc., from such publishers.

The Society of Authors engaged their own lawyers, and took on every case of malpractice. At the present moment, they are fighting, tooth-and-nail, to obtain a quick installation of the Public Lending Right bill, and get better returns for the authors.

My new book "What Pimbo Did Next!" was well under way, with sales on a par with those of "Pimbo". Usually, I tried to arrange for my book's publication, to be around October, giving me three months of Christmas sales. So far, including my first two books, I had made sales of almost fifteen thousand copies, pounding the beat, was hard work, but, the fact that people were purchasing something that you had created, softened the blow, especially when they tell you how much they enjoyed your last book.

Customers were really wonderful. "I heard you were about", "My mum told me you'd been around to her". "I thought it was your time to be around", "Ah, good. It's you, you're usually around for me to get my grandchildren a book for Christmas", and so it went on. At times I felt like the match-stick painter, Lowery, with flat cap – but instead of painting, I stood at the factory gates, putting it into words.

One lady, really surprised me, at her call to "Come in!" I found that she was upstairs. "You'll find my handbag in the sitting room, first on the left, help yourself, I can't come down I'm in the bath!" came a steamy voice from the bathroom. "I like your books, I got in a row from the kids, because I missed you last year!"

An old man amused me. After doing my usual spiel, he said, between gulps of tea. "Well, I know you come around every year, leave the book with me, and I'll let you know next year if I want it!" The amazing thing was – he really meant it!

Eventually, however, came the inevitable. Someone was after me! It came as a letter one morning. "Dear Mr. Unwin, I think what you have written about my husband is disgraceful. I have been to Burlington Press, and asked them to stop printing further copies. Also, I am going to the local paper, so that your writing about my husband, is made public, if you do not withdraw all copies of your book, I shall take the matter further in the High Courts. Signed, Mrs. X and Son."

Now, the amazing thing was, that, I had praised her husband for his integrity, good spirits, pointed out his popularity among Cambridge folk, and remarked that his sudden death, had left a lot of friends behind.

Instead of going on my sales-round, I decided on seeing the good lady, immediately. It's the last thing a salesman wants, to have any problem on his mind, when seen at the door. He must present himself as a confident trouble-free personality, whose one desire is to satisfy his customer.

The letter writer came to the door, seconds after my knock. As soon as I mentioned who I was, and the purpose of my visit, she slammed the door shut – with my finishing the conversation through the uplifted letter-box. I pointed out that I had written nothing but praise about her late husband, if, in anyway, I'd offended her, well, then, I was sorry, but, I had no intentions of withdrawing my book from sale to the public.

On returning home, I wrote immediately to the Society of Authors, asking their advice, and to know the ins and outs of the libel law; I explained the entire story to them, actually cutting out the excerpt from the chapter, that mentioned the husband, and sending it with the letter. Almost by return post, they sent me a reply, and a pamphlet on libel law.

In a kind letter they explained the following points:

You cannot actually libel a *dead* man!

But, should what you say, be detrimental to the welfare of the next of kin, i.e. shop-keeper, whereby the quality of his father's stock is criticized, thus, making it difficult for the son to carry on the business, this is deemed as an infringement of the libel law.

The existence, name, and death of the unfortunate husband, is an historical fact, there is *no* infringement of the libel law! The Society went on the say, that in their view, the woman had no cause to bring any such case to court. They suggested that I forward a solicitor's letter to her

Woman in country house

immediately.

One point in her letter, which the Society brought out, was that she had signed it, Mrs. X. and Son. It was hardly likely, that a son, would hide behind his mother's letter, especially as his father had received such a good write-up.

I made another call to the woman. This time, she kept the door shut, making her torrent of abuse at me from the letter-box. Waiting patiently until the diatribe had finished. I went to town on her. Finishing with the threat, that if she did not stop her silliness, I would take her to court, and she might have to cough-up a large amount of money through damages!

Apparently this did the trick! I heard no more from her. A few weeks later, I met her in the street, she was walking her dog. Venturing a "Good morning", brought nothing but an icy stare. Each year, when selling in her vicinity I tried to communicate with her, until, to my delight she replied with "A bit cold though, for the time of year!"

I suppose, really, the death of her husband, had given her such a shock, that in sheer frustration, she'd taken it out on me. Maybe, she had a guilt complex about whether or not, she might have been a better wife – who knows. But, it had me going for a time!

Burlington Press had done a good job on my new book. It was in paper-back, in order to keep the price down. Going around a working estate, with a book priced at anything above £2, would be completely negative. Janet, had done some nice drawings, and made the book come to life! As, is usual, with a new book out, you were asked to do Radio interviews.

These were good fun, for instant realism, the interviewer would enact the whole scene as though I were at the door of a customer. With the tape running, I would rap at my door, with my daughter taking over the role as housewife. With one of us, usually bursting out laughing, we had quite a few takes!

Carol West, one of my first interviewers, was marvellous at putting me at ease. One point, usually coming out was, "Mr. Unwin. Self-styled author!" I soon laid this ghost, by pointing out that I was now a paid up member of the Society of Authors – the old enemy Ego, cropping up again.

Doing an interview with a young girl cub reporter at my local paper's office. I noticed that during the interview, the young lady kept turning to gaze at the "Staff" door. Eventually, a young girl of similar age came through, at which, my interviewer shouted out, for all in the foyer to hear, "Don't forget you owe me £2", then, coolly carried on with my interview.

Making sure that my 5,000 copies of each run-off were sold before my new book came out, was, at times a pressure, mainly, because I had to make sure that the money was in, to pay for my current book. Buses, were my usual form of transport, but, going out to outlying villages, and sticking to my quota of sales, could be a challenge!

One day, with just two books needing selling, I could see the approaching bus which would take me home. Knowing that the next bus wouldn't be along for over an hour, I still stuck to my quota.

On selling the remaining two books, I made my way on the mile journey to the bus stop, only to be told that it had been "taken off" – there would be no more buses that day!

Walking to the main road from the village, a distance of four miles, I was able to catch a bus to Cambridge, almost immediately. But my joy was short lived, the bus, came under the new regulations, which sent it on a round-a-bout course, around all the outlying villages, picking up school children as well as adults.

The whole journey set me back two hours. For the sake of my quota, instead of getting home by 5 pm, it turned out to be 7 pm, with a worried Jenny awaiting my return. Such is life!

Doing my rounds in the Winter wasn't bad. I could keep warmer, much better than I could keep cool in Summer. Rain, that is driving rain, was my worst enemy. Ordinary drizzle, would be offset by rain-proof equipment, keeping my books dry was of major importance. Looking through the window to see if it had stopped raining, going out when it had and then having to come back again on a fresh downpour, was hard work. So, usually I kept out until I could manage no longer to keep dry – then call it a day. My brush selling and milk round had steeled me for such ventures.

In many ways it was an adventure. Reaching a village where I'd never been before, on a wet dismal day, augured, not *too* well for sprightly sales. The local paper, having a radius of say, twenty five miles, meant that people in the village, had heard about my books. By this means, I was adding to my readership, with an eye for future sales. I found the village folk, wonderful. Many of them had had past experience of Cambridge. They did a large amount of reading, and I found interesting comparisions, between the mythical acceptance that "Townies" did more reading than country folk. In literary journals, I'd read that of three people going into a book store, one purchased, one stole, and the other browsed. Each year, I found, that many more, than literary pundits expounded, were likely to enjoy reading literature, of these very few ever entered a book shop, these people I was ferreting out!

I was still getting many requests for help in getting people started on the writing trail. Some shared the manuscripts they had written. One old lady, in a magnificent country house, it must have cost thousands a year for heating bills, kept me waiting at the door for minutes on end. I could hear a puffing and blowing so waited expectantly. She was walking with the aid of a Zimmer, wearing a black shawl, she seemed like a character from Dracula.

On her invitation, I walked through a musty hall, saw through to the kitchen, the servants' bells, now hanging limp, and rusting, from the decaying board on the wall.

The kitchen had a brick floor, the table, now yellow, but, no doubt scrubbed white in the olden days. But, not for me, the kitchen, I was shown into the reception lounge, dark, musty smelly curtains, cobwebs galore.

Once seated, the old lady got down to business. Producing a dog-eared yellow book, she handed it to me. "This is the original manuscript of an old

German fairy tale which was made into a famous opera – The Nut Cracker Suite. It is priceless, I would like to get it published into English – can you do it for me?"

She spoke in clipped broken English, with a gutteral accent. The old lady, seemingly was of German origin. Having studied a little German during my war stint, I deciphered a few words here, and there. "It would have to be translated, this would make the project a costly affair!" I told her. "The market for such a work, would be a specialised one, which makes it very limited in sales. Only a publisher with money to burn, would chance his arm on such a venture!"

"But, you! Could you do it, I'll pay you fifty pounds?"

Taking in the surroundings, the dear old soul, hadn't any idea of the value of money. She was living in the past. Copies of "Argosy", "Blackwoods" and "Harpers" magazines, were lying around, yellow, and with wilting pages. I hadn't any idea of the potentiality of the manuscript for making money. Maybe I was throwing away a fortune, and yet, there may be thousands, and thousands of similar copies lying around in Germany as museum pieces.

Explaining to the old lady the futility of it all, I thanked her, and took my leave. On the way out, for the first time, I noticed the mansion was up for sale. Well clear of the great building, I looked up at the decaying walls, the missing tiles high up on the roof, the only solitary T.V. aerial, the only anachronism belying the whole set up. I thought then of the wonderful world I had let myself into.

Not knowing from day to day, whom I might meet.

The following year, when I made my call, the mansion had been sold, small vans were littered everywhere; roof tilers, glaziers, builders, plumbers, landscape gardeners. The place was undoubtedly worth a fortune, and it would cost a fortune to get it into shape. I reckon the dear old lady would turn in her grave at the thought, her fifty pounds would not have gone beyond moving the T.V. ariel!

So, through the pleasantries of the Spring weather, through to the golden hedges of Autumn, and thus into Winter, I plied my trade of book selling. Receiving letters, phone-calls, calls for further copies of those now out of print.

It was difficult for me to have reprints done, with my target of a book a year, it was uneconomical for me to go round again, selling a book I'd already been along with.

However, on the strength of the insistent demand, I had a few hundred of each printed and went round in between my usual calls, this caused a little confusion, and a great deal of hard work, with my just breaking even in the shops, and gaining as little as 10p on each copy.

With sales of "What Pimbo Did Next" nearing the allotted 5,000, I began my third book, "Pimbo and Jenny in Old Cambridge". Usually, it took me about three months to write a book, without my door-to-door calls, I could manage one in a month. The Cambridge tag was used by me to attract the tourist trade. They liked to go back carrying a memento of their visit.

The price of the paper back was £1.75p. The

unit cost gave me enough margin of profit to enable me to make sure that I would be able to launch my new book. The Burlington Press were very good to me, allowing me to pay for the books as I sold them. Usually, a once monthly substantial cheque did the trick, with the Press storing the books, and when required delivering them to my door. I was learning each year, the plight of the literary world, with its drop in book sales, higher printing costs, but somehow through the Grace of God, I kept going!

CHAPTER 9

I'll Walk Down the Avenue because I haven't got a Car

Jenny, by now was getting deeper into her arthritis. Mr Murley, her Consultant, was looking after her well, to the extent of a pair of new knee-joints, and having her finger broken to allow the slipping in of nylon, for replaced tendons. Pain, was the bug-bear of the whole illness, many times Jenny would wake in the night to sit sobbing with the excrutiating pain. Years back, we used to laugh at her insisting on having a travelling rug over her knees in warm weather. We, now knew it was the beginning of the attack, which spread insidiously into every joint.

But, she was very brave. She wouldn't let my worry about her, interfere with my book-sales, "You've come so far", she'd say, "and you're not giving up until you've written at least twelve books!"

In the local paper, I read of a person being found dead in a house which had just been converted, from a set of cottages. It was in a different village to that of my autobiographical customer, with the £1,000. I wondered if there was any link-up? Life, is indeed, stranger than fiction!

My new book contained many anecdotes concerning characters of long ago. On my rounds, doting daughters had told me lovely snippets from their dad's lives, as did, sons, concerning their mum's. Many of them I actually knew from my school-days. I wrote on the principle that people in those days were real characters, they *had* to be in order to survive. Nowadays, a "character", usually, is a person who has had a love life, as that of a rabbit, let down woman, after woman, drunk, or drugged himself silly, for this, he gets prominent features in every National newspaper, and T.V. interviews, until his face is as familiar as the sitting room furniture!

At one door, I was asked by a rather "La-di-dah" male. "How do you manage to write, with a mere Elementary School education? Without being rude, I reminded him of a George Bernard Shaw anecdote! Congratulating a young man, on the success of his first novel, Shaw was told by the up-and-coming author, that he intended working his passage around the world, which, G.B.S., thought excellent. The young writer, added, that he would then go on to University.

"What," came the reply, "and interrupt your education?"

This is, of course, the answer to many, who ask at the door "Could *I* write stories. I make up lovely bed-time stories for my children – but, I went only to an ordinary school?"

Of course they can write stories, go to it, you care-worn, nappy folding little Cinderellas, *go* to the Ball. I read in a literary journal, that an essay, written by a public-schoolboy in perfect English grammar, would be as dull as ditch water. This wasn't of course to belittle grammar, sloppy writing is not a pretty sight.

But it's the life breathed into the creation that counts. God, when He made Man, with the lifeless bone structure before Him, actually, had to bend down and *breathe* life into Man!

It reminded me, too, of an old retired mariner who lived on the outskirts of Brighton. By the moon, the tides, the wind, the behaviour of birds, the insects in the hedges, the behaviour of wildlife, and the accumulation of his own adventures travelling the High-seas, could give an answer to many of life's problems – and could tell the weather better than anyone. His advice was sort by the thousands of people who visited him from far and wide.

All this, reached the ears of a certain University Research Unit, doing a project on Human Behaviour. They visited the old man, offering him a large sum of money to spend six-months with them, while they carried out a research on him, to find out what made him "tick". A little reluctantly, he went off with them to their University laboratories.

He was back within a fortnight! His answer to those who asked him, "what went wrong?" was, "They muddled me up – I couldn't think straight!"

This true story was published by "Reader's Digest" some years ago.

"Pimbo and Jenny in Old Cambridge" was full of such like characters. "One-off" people, who caused others to laugh with them, not at them. A certain character named "Sluice Parker" filled the bill! "Sluice", would travel round from house to house selling house plants. He would remove a plant from the front garden of his customer then go to the back door to sell it. Remarking "It'll go well with your one in the front garden!" Other ruses of the lovable old rascal were to sell a plant in its pot (usually, with no root). When confronted with his misdemeanor, by an irate housewife, "Sluice" would ask in a professional tone, "Did you water it?" This, of course was a "tails you lose, heads, I win" type of question, with a two head penny, as "Sluice's" defence!

Poor old "Sluice", had repeated confrontations with the local magistrate, owing to his drinking habits. On one occasion, the magistrate sentenced him to "seven days, for disorderly conduct!" To the amusement of the court, our hero, replied, "Does that mean nights as well, Sir?"

As a sure sign of "Sluice" Parker's popularity, tales of his exploits will be bandied around for years to come, almost in a folk-legend category.

Moving around from door to door, village to village, built up inside me a vast store of experience, with people, places and all the little quirks of human nature. Many writers have to spend years on research, before they can attempt to write a book.

I wasn't getting mine free, but, as a Hoover "advert" might claim, "I get it as I walk, as I reap, as I glean!"

Going from door-to-door, after a few years, taught me many things. Checking up the washing on the line!

Were there signs of young children, was the

linen of a quality, that suggested affluence. Trendy underwear, go-go, track suits for the young husband, suggested a couple that would be interested in the localities history!

Too many plants in the window, the inevitable aspidistra, the old cat sitting on the window sill depicted an old pensioner occupant. A new angled lamp, sitting on the table overlooking the front garden, could be the home of an Insurance-man, a person, well versed in keeping his own accounts, or, perhaps a fellow writer, or student.

The state, and amount of milk bottles on the doorstep. Around the four or five mark, a fairly large family, maybe two children. A solitary bottle, beautifully washed out, standing on a little ceramic mat, told maybe of a prissy housewife, who, might not take too kindly to a door-to-door salesman.

Newspapers, be they tabloids, or the "Manchester Guardian", "Daily Telegraph", or "Times", each, told a political story of the occupant inside. Stuffed in the letterboxes, spoke of occupants having a lie in, or out at work. I found some people were *never* in. I've been on a doorstep as early as 8 a.m., returned at 6.30 p.m., to find the householder still not at home. One, thing, I am convinced of, is, that should the housewife be unable to take on a part-time job, the economical state of many homes would be in a catastrophical condition. I take my hat off to the lady of the house, who, combines looking after her children, with helping towards the home's financial burdens.

During an interview with John Gaskell, I was asked how I felt about walking around the stately homes of England, selling my book, to all, and sundry. I offered him a little analogy, using the Judy Garland, and Gene Kelly dance scene, where they sing, "Then we'll walk down the avenue, yes, we'll walk down the avenue, we'll walk down the avenue, because we haven't got a car!"

It was seeing this in print, the day after the interview, that Jenny suggested that I buy a car. "You won't have to rely on buses, sometimes, you're two hours late from the time you would have been home with a car!"

Jenny was right! It would help too, when taking her to hospital for her regular appointments with Mr Murley. The Voluntary Car service was a grand innovation, but, sometimes, a two hour wait for a car to arrive in order to take her home was very taxing on her health, and temper!

At the present moment the Society of Authors were putting up a great fight in it's P.L.R. campaign for authors. Through the letters, received by writers, the Journal exposed all the frailties of the writing world.

Maybe, I was lucky, not to have to rely on the whims of publishers, and booksellers, who had not "done right" by their bread and butter supplier! But, I felt for those of a similar ilk to myself, maybe, receiving monies for rights of allowing a book to be borrowed from a library wasn't expecting too much!

Very few people at the door, would ever mention library books. Should they do so, it was on the lines of "Oh! I always get my books from the library!" I'm sure they didn't understand the issue, because, showing such little concern for the

Ex-headmaster of Leys School, painting

author, seemed out of context with their personality. Pensioners, of course, were a different category.

Reading through debates about P.L.R. (Public Lending Right) in the larger newspapers, I was surprised to find a lack of knowledge among both M.P.s and Civil Servants, of the problems a struggling author goes through – it seemed that neither did they care.

In fact, I recognised the names of three M.P's, who *were* authors, and yet fought against the P.L.R. Moral convictions, and vote catching, in this case, were poor bedfellows!

On my journeys, I met a fellow writer with a strange story to tell. Having sent a novel to a certain publisher, he was told that the work was very promising. There was little doubt that he had considerable talent. He was asked to put in a little revision, and try again.

His second effort was returned with the comment, "Your future promise as a writer, does not fulfil your early work. Somewhere, along the line, your talent has evaporated into nothingness!"

In mentioning these little snippets, I think it important that the lay reader understands what goes on behind the scenes of the writing world. It is no way meant to disparage publishers and book-sellers. When a book is published, a lot of lay people think the author has made it to Mecca. They visualise queues of patrons lining the pavements to purchase the book.

I think it better, the would-be-author should know all about the smaller writers, who, have to struggle in order to make a semblance of a living. In this respect, I'm glad that I've gone the way I have. Through a gradual process, I've been vicariously through the pangs of a disappointment that the ordinary author relying on the integrity of his aides, goes through.

Not for me devastating reviews which could knock the author clean out of the writing world. My reviewer is the person that buys a book from me at the door!

"I enjoyed your last book, hope this one's as good!"

"Why don't you bring "Pimbo" up-to-date!" (a point I straight away worked on).

As I was walking along a certain street in Cambridge, a large lorry pulled up alongside the kerb. The driver, leaning out of his cab window, called me across to him.

"'Ere mate. Are you the geezer what wrote "What Pimbo Did Next?""

On my confirmation of this query, he went on, "I ain't never been much of a reader. But, I was held up at the docks the other week, all night it was. I found your book in the cab, I read it from start to finish. Never thought I could read a book through, myself, mate! Call round me mum's again, she'll buy another one! She must have popped it into the cab for me!"

I felt what a *good* review it was! The main thing being that this chap, no great shakes as a literary genius had enjoyed reading my work. It augers well for the thousands of would-be-authors, who think their work not good enough to be accepted. Also, the point that I've found out most important of all, is, that there are thousands, and thousands, of readers, that never visit a bookshop, waiting in their homes, looking for an author!

Then again, on my rounds, I'm able to gauge the pulse of the reader, what they like to read, what makes them laugh, what makes them cry.

One lady in her home, told me that in every one of my books, she had found something to cry about, quite pleased about it, she was. Of course I try a little bit of manipulation, "Which chapter did you like best?" Many is the time when the reply has astonished me. The very chapter that I thought a weak link, turns out to be a strong link.

Visiting homes, had been a feature of my life for at least thirty years. Brush salesman, milkman, colporteur, I've seen children I gave little tins of polish to, as a brush salesman, grow up, get married, then purchase a book from me for their own children.

Also, it gives you confidence. I've been into homes of the well-to-do as well as the poorest of the poor. Invited into the home of the ex-Leys School, Headmaster, he proudly showed me the paintings, he always did, when on holiday in the States, Greenwich Village, I think it was. They were lovely.

"Never written a book, that is, a novel!" he rather sadly pointed out, "One thing I'd liked to have done, you're lucky, my boy!"

I've had plenty of laughs at the door. A lady asked me if I ever carried second lines, that is, another product as well as my book. Pointing out that I had not, and didn't believe in doing so, I asked her why?

It seemed that her old brush salesman of many years ago, made a habit of selling other products, as well as his own. Should he not sell a brush, out would come a mail order catalogue. If this failed, a tempting line of lisle stockings were presented. Football coupons, raffle tickets, bingo dockets, nothing escaped his commercial eye. The trouble was, that once a housewife spotted him coming down the path, they never opened the door to him. It look too long for him to display his wares, and proved much too expensive a demonstration at that!

With "Pimbo and Jenny in Old Cambridge" going well, I made plans for my next book which would be entitled "From Cambridge – One and All". It was a story about the young men of Cambridge and its Shires, who volunteered to join the colours in the early stages of the War. Realising that most war stories were of gallantry and sacrifice, usually from officers and N.C.O.s, I thought it would be a change to use as heroes, young men with ordinary backgrounds, that never experienced much in the glory stakes, but, never-the-less, stuck it out, in the grime and sand of the desert.

The unit I joined was made up of volunteers from the Cambridge areas. Joshua Taylor, son of one of the largest store owners in the City, was among the first to join. Billy Rickaby, the Newmarket jockey, Harry Wragg, his fellow rider, and many local celebrities were among the little band, the main body coming from the work force. Keeping up with my book-a-year plan was not easy. My writing time would come from after my daily selling routine. Leaving my home at 7.45 a.m., in order to avoid traffic jams, I usually was on my first doorstep at 8.30 a.m. It was the time that many harrassed mothers were getting ready their offspring for school. Occasionally, a mother just couldn't cope with me at the door, and handle her boisterous youngsters. But, on the whole, I found this period between 8.30 a.m. and 9.00 a.m. a more productive time. People, I would never have seen after 9 a.m., were able to purchase a book.

My selling day could go on until around 2.30 p.m., making my walking stint a six hour sojourn. After a little snooze, I was back at the writing desk.

Much has been written in literary Journals about the various methods authors find beneficial to their cause. Some preferred shutting themselves away in a private atmosphere, others, too, found it impossible to write under pressure of noise, and domestic interference.

Myself, I am quite happy to write anywhere. People talking in my presence whilst writing, do not disturb me, unduly. Early morning, I find the best time. My mind is clear and fresh, themes, plots, and characters, thought up over night, pop out fresh and dusted in the morning.

In my early days, I did a reasonable amount of revision, but, as I grew more confident, this grew less.

First thoughts, I find, usually are the best thoughts, they don't need revision.

Roget's Thesaurus, a must for most authors, I read avidly in my early days. Nowadays, I use it only as a dictionary. It's a magnificent work but, I find choosing a word outside your own vocabulary, cuts out a little continuity, like slipping in a false note, to a musical piece!

I advise any would-be-authors to read everything they can lay their hands on. Never try to copy another writer's style, if you can't get by on your own talent – others won't help. Be yourself – and don't be afraid of it – you're as good as anybody when you write about real people, and real life.

CHAPTER 10

I Meet Con-Men

A phone call one morning, gave me hope, that someone was willing to take over a considerable part of my book distribution. Going round to the given address, I found two bright young men awaiting me. Outside, their rather small terraced-house, stood a smart looking delivery van.

"We've heard a lot about you, Mr Unwin!" one of the men, said with warmth, "I think we can curtail a little of your pavement bashing!" The other man proffered me a card. Boulton Bro's Ltd. Book Distributors.

"What have you, on offer?" I asked a trifle dubiously. My thoughts ran to what I'd read about literary agents and their commission charges (quite rightly so), but unless you really are "raking it in" it *would* take away a large slice of the earnings.

"What's your run-off?" the elder of the two asked. On my reply, he looked across to his brother, then back to me.

"You'll have to up it to 10,000, it's chicken feed at the moment you know!"

This sounded good to me. It would be the

equivalent of my books going through the ordinary channels, with me sitting back, waiting for the cash to roll in. There had to be a catch somewhere!

"How do you, work, what's the score?" I asked.

Offering me a drink, the younger man leaned across to me.

"Now look here, Mr Unwin. So far you've gone it alone. Right? There's no reason why your books can't be made Universal, they're read in schools, stored in libraries all over the country, I've done my homework you know, I know all about you! Now listen, there's nothing "porny" in your stuff, it can be read by kids just off the dummy *and* the geriatrics, pardon my expression. It's a family book, not too many of them going the rounds, you know!"

Watching me nodding my approval, the other man joined in.

"Another thing, you're selling 125 books a week, your local rag prints a list of best-sellers each week, sent in by the book-shops. Now, let's be honest, how many books sell more than 125 per week, every week, that is?" Noticing my rapt attention, he finished "You're a best seller in your own back yard, but what's stopping you from doing it on a bigger scale. Take your "Dew on my Feet", how many people know what goes on inside a loony-bin. All over the country, people would love to know, you were *there*, they've got it straight from the horses mouth – !"

"You still haven't told me the score!" I said!

"All right! You have a ten thousand run-off, right. You hand over 5,000 to us for distribution. We've got the low down on shops, libraries, schools, hospitals. We travel all over the U.K., we place your books in all these places, you pay us twenty per cent of the "starting price". You may not see us for a year – in the meantime, *you* can be selling the rest of the run-off – it can't be bad, can it?"

I was thinking deeply. Getting money from book-sellers, libraries, could be a long time affair. Not that they wouldn't pay, but, it was *when* would they pay?

The printer had to be paid. Could I afford to wait, maybe, for a year, before I could settle his bill? Also, the commission would take away my already lean profit on the books – !

"I don't know, I can't give you an answer right away, I'll have to think it over – you'll have to give me time!"

The men's expressions changed somewhat. "We can't afford to wait. We're leaving here tonight, if you can't make up your mind, it'll be too late. Why not let us take a few thousand of your current book, give us a try?"

Being a salesman, I recognised this as high pressure selling. Any salesman, with a good product to sell, doesn't need to resort to such methods of selling. I had visions of my handing over the books, and perhaps never setting eyes on books, or salesmen again. They, maybe, had hundreds of bookshops, that might pay cash for half-a-dozen copies, but, spread over the country, 5,000 books would soon be sold, and, they would be very much richer.

I have never expected writing to be an easy touch, door-to-door selling suited me fine. No hassle, no unpaid bills, an intimate touch with a reader's need, no waiting for the slim envelope to plop onto the mat! Maybe, these two young men *were* honest. Perhaps, like myself, risking their arm on a new venture. Well, then, they were young enough to take my refusal as water off a duck's back!

I said "No, I'm sorry. Good of you to give me the chance. But, I'll stick to my own distribution. O.K.?"

On my way home, I looked back at the house. It was in a crowded street, cars, cycles littered the area. I remembered as a boy nearly every house had a maid. Now, sub-lets, abounded, six-or-seven to a house, the place had deteriorated. On a later visit, curious as ever, I saw, whom, I thought to be the landlord of the house where I had visited the two would-be-distributors. I inquired of their whereabouts, pretending I wanted to do business with them.

"Don't mention those two sharks to me!" came the reply, "skipped off without paying the rent, took money from the gas meter – you're lucky they didn't catch *you*!" An unfair "distribution" of wealth, I thought, not in the least desirable – in *my* "book"!

Reading through various literary papers, I found that many publishers, and authors, were turning their eyes out to the far off lands for new markets, Japan, China, India, were among the chosen customers. Noticing a meeting, due, at the Bookman's Club, I attended it, to find out more about the new innovations.

Before the lectures, rounds of drinks, brought

out the slick, professional aspects of those present. Eyes, glinted with pride, as one told another of the present trends in both printing and book selling. Binding of books, held court, sewing, adhesion, gum, and cross binding, being the jargon of the moment.

Further talks, made it clear that the future of the novel might well be in the amazing era of the computer. Plots, characters, dramatic situations, fed into the electronic wonder, would out do anything as writer may cook-up.

The opening lecture was given by a young, go-ahead, ex-editor of a once glossy journal. His job was to sell books abroad. In parternship, with a similarly bright young man, they arranged packages, wrote, edited, and printed their own books.

"We're packages, you could say! But we spend money on a project that even large publishers would be unable to cope with. Middlemen, yes in a way, but we earn our money by finding new markets abroad, Japan, Finland, Canada, China.

It's possible that we might spend two years preparing a specialist book, incidently, we find do-it-yourself books the most popular!"

After a few questions, he went on. "Our success is due to the money spent on preparation. We then rely on fairly substantial orders by, say, ten or a dozen overseas publishers, which, in the end, make up one large sale in the U.K. Reprints are fairly common, and after six years hard work, our annual turnover is in the region of two million pounds!"

Leaning across the lecturer's table, he produced

a long black folder. In concertina fashion, unrolling it, produced a kind of elongated picture album. This "book" consists of four hundred and fifty pages. Here, in this album, are a similar amount of mock-up pictures, of what the "book" contains. This gives the publisher an exact replica of the "book", which, back in England, although not in print, I'm ready to produce for immediate shipment.

Should you study the drawings, you'll find the majority are a mere duplication!" Pointing to half-a-dozen pictures in the centre of, the album, he went on. "These are the only ones in continuity, they actually show a do-it-yourself window repair in action. So you see, what I'm doing, is selling a "book", not yet printed, my *own* money is at stake. Quoting a delivery date to coincide with the "books" production, I'm handed over a fair sized monetary deposit, and move over to my next client!" I sat spell-bound – selling a book before it was written – well!

After a round of applause for his expositions, he picked up a large well illustrated book on photography.

"Selling at seventeen pounds, this book has made the author famous overseas. Amazingly, he didn't write a word of it, we did it ourselves – just used his remarkable photographs!"

The young man wasn't finished. He held up another large volume. I failed to catch the title, but it sounded something like "Self Sufficiency".

"This book I never rated! A complete fantasy, all about how to manage on a desert island should one become shipwrecked. I did the rounds, using the theme, "Fantasies in reality", but no one would touch it. Then, one day, hey presto, a small back room publisher in Germany, fell in love with it. It turned into a best-seller for him – I now call it "Reality in fantasies!"

Came a further bout of questions which were answered smoothly and honestly by the younger lecturer.

"Yes I do think America is *the* place in which to sell books!" "Yes, I made sure that consignments *were* delivered by the deadline!" "Translations, I left to the country concerned, I hadn't the expertise to deal with technical books!"

"No, sharp practice, didn't come into it. Should I sell an idea, instead of the actual book, well then, I regarded that, as a commission, and made sure of its completion!"

"No, I didn't look upon myself as a pirate, merely cashing in on a wide open market – *any* book could make best seller, if only it were "Sold" in the correct hyping technique!" "Yes, maybe the author, in years to come, would emerge as the ball, tossed between publisher and agent!"

"Yes, the novel could be on the way out, sold to the micro-chip and new computer techniques!"

The young man closed his address by bringing out the importance of looking back at the best-seller, then, to find a new writer to take over the mantle of the previous author. Quoting the popularity of the Dr. Brooks' series, he told of his ferreting out a promising young housewife living in London, who, gave him a synopsis on a potential book on "Baby Care".

Getting together, his partner and he, thrashed

out the idea with the authoress. The end result being another best seller, which, so far, has been translated into fourteen languages!

I left the meeting in a daze. The book world was indeed, a place for the young pioneers. Little did I realise when peeping into the tranquility of Heffers, Galloway and Porter, and Bowes and Bowes, that such things went on outside those premises. But, I was pleased about the young housewife, with her book on "Baby Care" it spoke "Volumes" for other would-be-authors.

My journey around the houses brought me many smiles. One dear old lady, arriving at the door with a walking aid, asked "Well, what's the book about my man?" I explained that I wrote about lots of characters, some, whom, she may well have known, ending up with, "I take you all around the little back streets!"

The old dear stood aghast. "But, my dear man, I can't walk far, I could never manage it!"

A few days after my attendance at the Bookman's Club, I read an article concerning overseas publishing. It seemed, that even in this field, things weren't all that rosy. A Canadian book critic, after reading a chapter of a certain British book, tried to buy a copy at eight different Canadian book-shops. Although, the distributor was in the employ of a well known British publisher, and held in high esteem in Canada, the search for the book proved fruitless.

A similar fate befell that of a special award winning book, in fact, the Booker Prize. Before winning the award, the book was unobtainable in any of the bookshops in Canada. After winning the prize, even then, only 1,000 copies were dispatched from England.

It seems that companies cannot risk a lot of money bringing in thousands of copies, they are not sure of selling. So they settle for very few, or even none at all!

Arriving home one evening the phone rang. To my delight it was Anglia T.V., they wanted an interview concerning my latest book, "From Cambridge, One and All". A Mr. John Kiddy was in charge. It was all very exciting, as my Hostel was in the centre of town, a good deal of the interview taking place with my little entourage following me around the Market Square.

Very conveniently, my book was on display in Bowes and Bowes window. The usual questions were asked, how many sales from door-to-door had I achieved? How long did I intend to keep going? What was the title of my next book? John Kiddy asked me, had I any suggestion for further coverage? Remembering an old lady, who, once told me, she sat watching a German bomber on a moonlight night approaching the little street where she lived. The subsequent bomb, destroyed half the house, luckily she survived. John, suggested I got in touch with her, for an interview.

Sadly, during the preceding week, the old lady died, taking with her the memories of that devastating occasion. She finished her days in an old people's home, often, repeating her account of that fateful night to avid listeners – had she been alive, it would have been her first T.V. appearance!

Within two days of my Anglia T.V. stint, I received a letter from the Daily Mail money pro-

Con-men offerig to distribute book

gramme. Apparently, they'd heard of my exploits, and wanted my confirmation for a competition they were running. Naturally, I couldn't put pen to paper quickly enough, (the old ego again!) sending off a detailed account of what had happened to me during my quest for writing fame!

Within two weeks, I received that elusive slim envelope, – I'd won a magnum of Champagne, and a column in the Daily Mail's Money page on Wednesdays. A local photographer was sent to me, resulting in my parading up and down King's Parade at least a dozen times.

I was taken from all sorts of angles, other than standing on my head.

Then, it was back into my flat, for a repeat of snaps, but, this time, the photograph was of me sitting at a desk, with my books in the foreground. This one made it to the Money Mail pages!

With my ego working overtime, it was thrilling to see myself in a prominent position in the Daily Mail. The very title Money Mail, was a bit of a misnomer. It was supposed to represent someone who'd made it in the money stakes, I certainly, had not, so far, seen a great deal of money from my ventures! But, there are thousands of aspiring writers who would settle for just getting their names in print, and their books into homes, schools and libraries – money, didn't come into it!

I was more than grateful for what had happened to me, and I hope that many, many would-be writers will be able to achieve the same.

A little ironically, the magnum of Champagne was delivered to me, dumped at the bottom of a stairway, leading out into a busy street. It could be seen from the pavement, and scores of students passed it on their way to their rooms. But, honesty prevailed, it was untouched when I found it!

So the days went on. Plenty of letters from readers who remembered vividly the days I was writing about, also many letters from abroad. At one door, I received good news from a doting mother. Her daughter, she told me, had read each book I'd written, and couldn't believe, that such an ordinary person as myself, was able to "make it" into print.

This fact, inspired her to have a go. Her mother mentioned that the daughter had studied my style, and the things I write about, and tried to keep as near as possible with my method of writing, without losing anything from her own personality.

Entering a short-story competition in a very classy Woman's Journal, the young lady won first prize! I felt almost as proud as the winner herself, and her mother called me in to have a drink of sherry, to celebrate the welcome win!

Of course, not every letter was one of praise. A gentleman took me to task on the question of how many contestants took part in a certain colourful barrow race, held annually in the centre of the City.

Despite a good deal of research on my part, it was very difficult to obtain names of the contestants, as the barrow race was some fifty years since!

To make it exciting, in my account, I embellished a little with the characters involved, bringing in one, or two, of my own inventions, to colour the story. The letter was rather abusive, and dogmatic. I wrote back. "Dear Sir, Thank you for your very kind letter. Dick Turpin *didn't* ride Black Bess to York – but everyone willed him to! Best wishes, Fred ("Pimbo") Unwin."

CHAPTER 11

Mister! You Haven't Put My Name in the Book!

I received a visit from a middle aged woman, who, had recently lost her husband. She told me that for three years, she had been trying to break into print. "Could you help me, at least, show me where I'm going wrong?" She implored. Feeling sorry for her, I pointed out, that my type of writing might not suit her style. It was not for me, the historical costumed romance, or, the slick mystery thriller.

"I understand. I've been on a correspondence course, they were excellent, taught me everything, but getting into print, as you implied, they told me to write what I thought suited my particular talent!"

She had brought with her the entire documentation appertaining to the course. It was a magnificent folder, in which she kept all paraphanalia to do with the series of lessons, stories, and reviews.

I had to smile, really. To think of the millions of words bandied, juggled, shuffled into sentences, sliced into paragraphs, then widened out into chapters. All done to attract the awaiting reader, we had to make them cry, laugh, think, grumble, or, finally discard us.

The course, started off with a beautifully printed text concerning copyright litigation. It included overseas and inland regulations, developed by the Universal Copyright Convention. It pointed out, that, to obtain complete copyright protection for your work, your book was to be registered and renewed at the Copyright Office, Library or Congress before the end of 1986. This, is of course, for a book published in England, but protected, automatically, by copyright notice prescribed by the Universal Copyright Convention. It gave a total of 75 years for the books' copyright protection.

I was very confused at reading this conglomeration of words, but, realised, what a beautiful piece of psychology it all was!

A course student would obtain a terrific amount of confidence, when reading that the U.S. were prepared to protect her brain child from pervert plagiarists. It would be an added bonus for the Correspondence Course Officials, the pupil would think that many of its writers had gained enough kudos to merit copyright protection. It was all above board, of course, why shouldn't their pupils gain literary success?

Funny too, that many writers enjoying their first successes, think of anything *but* copyright!

The woman showed me her recent manuscript. I went over it with her, she had complied with all the course's instructions, there was a slight semblance of a beginning, middle, and end to her story. It was a lovely story, about a young man roaming the countryside, looking for work. Taking on a job here, and a job there. Descriptive passages came over well, and the story took on a nice easy James Stewart kind of casualness.

The young man was accused by the police of a robbery at a village store. His roaming nature, lack of finance had placed him at the top of the list of suspects, with the police only too willing to make a shut case of it!

Just as he was about to be sent to jail, the real culprit came to light! The wandering hobo was given a regular job, by a sympathetic lady in the village, thus, all ended well.

The manuscript had been rejected by six journals none of them, making any comment upon the merit of the story.

Looking across at the authoress, made me think of thousands, and thousands, of similar writers, yet, to break into print. I could well imagine them sitting back and thinking to themselves, well, this must be it!

On the surface there seemed nothing wrong with the story – so why was it rejected?

I pointed out immediately that she must not hold too much store on my previous success at writing stories. It might well, be, that should I submit a story of mine to a host of publishers, it could suffer the same fate as her own. One accepted story, does not mean the author has a monopoly over any other writer. I knew a writer-beginner, who, had success with his very first venture. It was three years after, before he broke into print again, and then only one article was accepted.

We went through her manuscript together, and came to the conclusion, with my pointing out, what we both ultimately agreed, were perhaps the story's main faults.

- It was a series of events, just linked together.
- The fact that the young man *was* able to exist on his casual work, made it difficult for the reader to really care what happened to him.
- There was no love interest, and the characters simply flitted, in, and out, of the narrative.
- The descriptive passages outweighed the story line.
- There was no depth in the story.
- The identity of the real thief was simply pulled from mid-air. There was no mention of him before his denoument. He should have had some conflict with the "hero" of the story, giving the reader a chance to become an armchair detective.
- All suspense, conflict came at the end of the tale, there seemed little motivation for the reader to reach that stage.

Ironically, I pointed out "Maybe, among another six Editors, the story might have 'clicked', sometimes, there seems no yardstick available to measure why one story gets the chop, and another succeeds!"

To my great delight, a year later, the "rejected suitor," called to thank me. She had done a good deal of revision on the story, sent it out again; on her fourth attempt, the story was accepted. One thing, I told her, success was due to her *accepting* criticism. Something that many beginners will *not* do, thousands of manuscripts lay on dusty shelves, simply because their creator won't swallow their pride. Sad to say, in my early days, I, too, was in that category!

Also, looking at other people's work, has a humbling effect. Often, the thought that "but, for the Grace of God," crossed your mind. You are looking at excellent work, that has not seen the light of day.

In my experience, a vital factor between success and failure, is Time. Many beginners rap out stuff far too quickly, maybe, on the false assumption, that their talent is so great, their inspiration out-weighing hard work, therefore, there is no need to spend a great deal of time "I took half-an-hour to write that poem!" They say proudly.

Many times, in my early days, I did just that! As I grew more experienced, mainly because my poems had achieved nothing, I began to put a lot more time writing a poem. As much as two hours could be spent on re-writing, twisting, turning, wrestling with words, in one short verse! Amazingly, the result was a simple unsophisticated poem, that to the eyes of the uninitiated, would seem small fry. But, I found the art of all writing, lay in the hard work put in, in order to disguise too much contrivation. It was the same in acting, really.

There is little doubt that a good deal of heart break exists among the many thousands of amateur writers. Most of which, never comes to the Editor's or public eye.

Maybe in the rat-race, the mice get trampled on, in the mad rush for acclaim.

A sad case came to my attention during my

selling rounds. The wife in question always invited me in for a cup of tea. Her husband, would leave his writing desk, to join in with me in our discussions about the fraility of the writing world. Harold was a keen would-be-author. "I've told my kids, that before I die I'm going to 'crack it.' One day, I'll become a published author!"

Looking at Harold's work, without being uncharitable, I could quite understand why he had accumulated so many rejection-slips. He'd defied all rules and regulations on how to become a successful writer – many points I had tried to help him with, had gone unheeded.

Harold, later contracted a painful terminal disease.

With his one good virtue, that of seeking out a suitable market, he wrote a long article, pointing out the rare disease he was suffering from, the excrutiating pain he had to put up with and the hope and fight against an unfavourable prognosis. The article was sent to a leading medical journal, which, luckily enough, was "looking into" the very disease which Harold had unfortunately contracted.

The only monies that Harold ever received, for his years of hard graft as a writer, came three days after his funeral – it was a cheque for ten pounds! On my next visit, his wife told me, sadly. "Allowing for the several days posting time, and the date on the cheque, you could say my husband died, as was his wish, a published author!"

The cheque was duly framed, and hangs above Harold's old writing desk. A testimony of the promise he'd made to his children!

Jenny's arthritis, in the meantime, was getting very much worse, hospital-wise, everything was being done to alleviate the pain. She was a brick to put up with my comings and goings, but, the work at the King's hostel kept her going, it was a kind of therapy on its own, having seven bed-makers under her command, a labyrinth of stairways to contend with, and the drug, and Garden House student's fracas, resulting to her never-say-die spirit. The 1968 days of the militant, almost taking over the College, gave me good material for my next book "In the Shadow of King's".

Then too, the low paid wages by the college, of which, the hostel keepers were the most vulnerable, needed fighting against, something, I intended to do.

My sales of books, door-to-door, had now reached a total of 35,000, working on the principle of a 5,000 run-off of five titles, plus "Pimbo" having reached the 10,000 mark. I was of course, very proud of the achievement, but, owe a lot to Jenny, in that she had sacrificed a good deal of my company for days of being alone during my selling sessions.

With the fact of Janet Simmonett being with child, the illustrator of my book "Gentle Tales of Old Cambridge" was Sarah Taylor, an excellent art teacher at the local college, her husband, working in a similar capacity at Impington Village College.

Sarah, had drawn a life-like picture of the City's renowned alcoholic. This man, when drunk, was a vile person, indeed, but, when sitting on the

Market, in a prominent position, a sweet smile for the kiddies, (all this, before his inebriation took hold) Trevor Hughes, was regarded by some as a "wonderful character". Indeed, to such an extent, that on his death, the colleges, clubbed together, giving him a televised funeral service.

Harolds writing desk and the framed £10 cheque

On my rounds with the book, a young student teacher tackled me about my writing of Trevor. "You didn't like the old man, did you – it came out in your writing?"

It wasn't that I didn't like him, it was the things he did. Time after time, he would receive specialised treatment, a new suit of clothes, and was given a fresh start.

"Trevor, wasn't an old man!" I replied. "The damage to his liver, and brain, made him an old man, he was under sixty when he died!"

"But, he was a character!" She insisted. "We can't write off characters in such a manner – we must learn to love them!"

My thoughts went out to the young people of the City, should they regard Trevor as a shining example to follow. Become an alcoholic, and get a state funeral! Then too, nurses I knew from my Addenbrooke's stint, had told me that nothing had been spared to save Trevor's life, he'd received exclusive V.I.P. treatment. I knew many hard working men in the back streets of Cambridge who had died from pneumonia – where a little extra treatment might have made their death more tolerable.

Still, maybe she had something, perhaps in years to come Fagin and Rasputin will become martyred Saints. It was fast coming that way, T.V. characters were thought more of than real people, at times. A few weeks ago a character from "Crossroads" "died", (only in the plot of course). Hundreds of people sent flowers for the funeral. Maybe, their neighbours a few doors away, had yet to receive bereavement honours?

The Stockwell saga was now well and truly sunk. John Gaskell, returning all the documentation I'd sent him, made a lovely gesture of reconciliation, adding, in his letter: "Best of luck with the book and your dealings with Stockwell. The contract seems to suggest that after 2,000 copies have been sold, you may purchase copies at a reduced rate!" (Much of the argument had been about Stockwell printing only 200 copies!)

Stockwell, in turn, made a nice reciprocal gesture. I had previously written to him to say that I would be taking on the selling of my own books. His reply, on par with John's, read. "We cannot help but feel concerned that you will be devoting your full time to selling your books. If your pension is sufficient to cover your living expenses, then we would feel less concerned. Please do let me know if I can be of further assistance to you! Best wishes."

I have, of course, kept every letter concerning the News and both parties. One day, maybe, I'll write a book about it. The amazing thing to come out of it all, was, the concern that both parties showed for me. The News were worried that I was about to be conned, and Stockwell's letter above, and many others showed a similar concern for my welfare. I suppose it's a lesson that *everyone* should read the small print, then turn over to the *other* side of the papers!

The Society of Authors for a bit of fun, and enlightenment, asked a few leading publishers for their thoughts on the perfect writer. To kick off, a quite erroneous statement attributed to Dr. Johnson gave a tone to the proceedings. "Sir, it is an undeniable fact, that, all writers are scoundrels. But publishers are a hundred times worse. They are fit for hanging by their ears from the tallest tree in Bloomsbury" (all tongue in cheek stuff, of course).

Christopher Sinclair-Stevenson (Hamish Hamilton) had this to say on what was expected of the perfect writer.

- Deliver the manuscript on time, and well typed.
- Keep to length and stipulated subject.
- Leave the jacket illustrations to publishers.
- Don't re-write in proof.
- Do not "invent" aunts and uncles, who have searched bookshops for your book in vain.
- Think of an unusual title.
- Say "thank you", now and then.
- Have faith.

From several expositions, Bertrand Russell came out as a most professional author. (Rayner Unwin. Allen and Unwin (no relation)) His work was perfectly expressed, and correct to the last comma. His relationship with his publisher was founded on mutual respect.

Carmen Callil (Virago) points out nicely to the impatient writers waiting for their royalty payments, that, thought, must be given to the publishing business founded in 1945 with a capital of £1,500. She agreed that an author would be rightly enraged at not receiving it when due on an arranged date, and expects interest above the bank rate for every day overdue!

All this of course has not affected me, and indeed is not likely to do so. But we must be thankful to literary journals, that they give writers, enlightenment to every aspect of their trade, be it the top notchers, or the little minnows.

After all, a book is only a book. It can be hyped, win talent awards, go to the top of the best seller list.

But, still thousands, and thousands, of people will never read it. They might judge it over their heads, just as a pub crowd sing lustily to "Roll out the Barrel", or a hushed Cathedral audience become enraptured with the Messiah, so will readers enjoy books of *their* choice.

My work went on, my goal of writing twelve books was yet a long way off. Thousands of people had purchased my books, something I never thought possible a few years ago. I would have laughed at anyone, had they told me that I would be signing thousands of books.

Mind you, it's not the same as standing in Foyles as purchasers mill around, or attending literary luncheons, where signatures are obtained.

But it's still a joy! It is my usual custom to put children's names in the "Pimbo" book, but I had left out the name of the youngest toddler. One day she came running across the pavement, dragged by her "big sister", crying her eyes out, "Mister, you haven't put *my* name in!"

Needless to say, you can't add anything to that. It made my day!

CHAPTER 12

We've Got to Pay the Rent

Many writers, I'm sure, get motivation at least in their early days, from reading about the struggles and strifes of fellow writers. Some, of course, think that genius will make up for hard work. It will, but so few of us are in the genius class.

My stimulus came from reading an account of Colin Wilson's struggle with his first book "The Outsider". Getting time to write was a serious problem. In those days paying the rent was something one had to achieve on his own, by the time rent was accounted for, £2, the rest of a £5 wage was used for food.

The author came to the conclusion that were there no rent to pay, he could afford, in his odd building job existence, to work a week, then have a week off, giving him time in which to write his novel. The problem was how could he do away with the need for paying the rent?

So, he bought a tent, and slept out under a tree in the open park. However, the tent was too visible and attracted on-lookers, so our hero settled for a sleeping bag. Thus, it was, that "The Outsider" was written, even then, after a long hard stuggle.

How many of us would sacrifice to that extent? Many correspondence courses even try to alleviate the burden of thinking up a plot! Looking through my old course lessons I came across a few. Now, these must be accepted in the spirit in which they are written. The pupil, pays to be taught, the method of writing a story. The course, tries to do its very best. Maybe the earnest young housewife, or, husband, has no idea at all, how to begin a story. The plot-a-day chart tried to overcome the problem.

Here is one example from an actual plot-a-day chart. Ginger, and Marmaduke, are almost identical cats, but Ginger loves to wander, whereas Marmaduke has a lazy, comfortable life with two, almost senile, old ladies. Marmaduke gets run over, but a friend of the old ladies, sees Ginger, and takes him to them. The old dears, in the dotage accept Ginger for their own cat. Ginger, of course, knowing when he's onto a good thing, plays up to the old ladies, and thereby has two homes.

Then too, plot ideas from true newspaper reports were graphed and given to the pupil writers:

(1) Engine driver Fred Jones knew something was wrong when he saw the diesel engine move off. For it was the day of the great rail strike.

(2) "My car lacks power," complains Mrs. T. Shaw, when she drove to the service station from Church in Savannah, Georgia, last night. She was told it *would* lack power, because she was towing a small foreign car, hooked to the rear bumper of her large saloon.

(3) Bert Benbow, and his race-mad family went out collecting their winnings. They had just pulled off the year's biggest betting coup, with their own racehorse at Worcester. At the end of three hours Bert and his family had collected £6,000 from about thirty betting shops scattered around several towns. (£6,000 in those days was a lot of money)

(4) "Arctic" death trudge and climb. The three climbers could see the light of safety, as they struggled down the mountain. But, Snowdonia, had become another Arctic. Deep snowdrifts, and hidden marshes, barred the way to their base hut!

(5) Dancer Pat Hurt was stranded – and scared, in a strange country. Then along came a Knight Errant in the shape of handsome Ben Coleman, staff sergeant, United States Air Force. He paid her fare back to Britain. And now Pat and Ben are to marry.

Twenty-one year old Pat, had gone to Turkey last march with a contract guaranteeing her £30 a week as a night club dancer in Izmir. Then, she found she was expected to act as "hostess" – but she refused. But she found she could not raise the money to buy back her contract and pay her fare home to Crew.

(6) The man who could not get married. Fireman Bruce Newman, of New York finds the call of duty stronger than the call of love. In the middle of his wedding ceremony, he dashed off with the best man to help put out a fire.

(7) Housewife Mrs. Cecil Dickins walked into her back garden the other night and found a chimpanzee sitting in the flower bed, and T.V. comedian Steve Allen up a tree. It was no new

experience said Mrs. Dickins. Now, she and her 50 residents who live near the Hollywood studios of actor Allen, have protested that outdoor scene shots for his nightly T.V. show are ruining their existence.

(8) When handyman Reg Stone started to build his six-room dream bungalow, he found in the middle of the proposed bedroom, towered a 32ft high electricity pole. While the Electricity Board bosses ponder what to do with the pole, Mr. Stone is building his bungalow around it.

The set of stories are all true. It's amazing to what lengths correspondence courses go to give satisfaction to their clients.

They come under a lot of abuse, a few of them undoubtedly deserve it. But, a would-be-writer will soon learn that a whole story can be built around a small theme. I was a clock repairer many years ago, and often had to go to customers' houses to wind, repair, or test out their clocks. One lady, I found very fussy, ever looking for faults, and calling me back. So, I built a story around her, having her as a young widow recently losing her devoted husband. The clock repairer was a good looking young man, who, at the time was dedicated to learning the trade. The young trainee was called to the house to repair the grandfather clock. Thinking he had made a good job of it, he was surprised to be called back after a few days, on the widow's complaint that the clock had stopped. This happened twice, on the third occasion, the young man marked the clock's position, knowing that it wouldn't stop, unless the case was moved. Almost in tears, the young widow confessed, her loneliness had got the better of her principle, she *had* deliberately moved the clock. She asked him, point blank "would he like to go out with her?".

He accepted, and later they were married!

It all sounds trite, but, I would like to add this little epilogue. The woman who typed the manuscript for me, (it was accepted) told me that it was one of my best efforts. Somewhere, someone, is ever waiting for a story to be written for them. They come from all walks of life. *Never* think your work is not good enough for them!

Another thing, the would-be-writer must always be on the look out for story lines that can be got from watching films. Listen to the dialogue, should you do this diligently you will be able to almost read the author's mind. True, it might affect the ending, you may well know what's coming. A lot can be learned about emotion, heart, pathos, and, also how to bring out character traits, without seeming to be trying!

In the film "Paper Moon" we have Tatum O'Neal refusing to go any farther in the car, because her so-called guardian insists on associating with a prostitute. In desperation the guardian of the young girl (Ryan O'Neal, her real father) sends the prostitute to talk Tatum round. The dialogue went something like this "Look kid! When I was fifteen, I had nothin' going for me. Nothin' up top (pointing to her breasts) and nothin' but a pair of skinny legs down below. By the time I was seventeen I was like the transformation of the ugly duckling, I was a beautiful young woman. Look, kid, I had to make up for those lost years. Now if you don't go along with me, you're gonner get nothin', I'm gonner get nothin', can't you see kid, I had no parents, like you, we've both gotta fight!"

The prostitute studies Tatum, who still refuses to budge.

In a softer voice, she goes on. "Tell you what, kid, maybe I'll make you up a bit, how'd you like that? A bit of powder, mascara, rouge, and I'll get you a little pair of brassieres, and maybe silk panties – now, what about it kid, are you coming?" Tatum's little face, for the first time breaks into a smile. She stands up, links arms with the prostitute and goes down to the car.

The writer in the dialogue, has touched upon Tatum's deep longing to become grown up. Despite her loathing the prostitute's way of life, she feels that she is the first one to help her grow up. The frailty of the "father" is brought out, too busy with his conning vocation, he has no time to think what the young girl is missing, no heart, no warmth, something missing in many families.

Then too with the lovely little cameo in "City Lights", Charlie Chaplin, has just been shown the transformation of the home which his lover has brought about. She shows him the lovely new curtains she's installed. Charlie gives her a loving kiss, walks across to the sink, washes his hands – then dries them on the curtains! Isn't that just like a man? But it goes deeper, Charlie had never been used to such luxury, all this brought out by action, not words!

Again in one film, Charlie gives a present to his girl friend's crippled brother – with a great hullabaloo the present is unwrapped – to reveal – a pair of skates! You need to be a skilled and brave writer to bring out such pathos in a comedy film. Also, it showed the sometimes lack of thought that men tend to show, when confronted with various aspects of the domestic scene!

Newspapers, films, T.V. sit-coms, represent a good breeding ground for story themes – but, of course, steer clear of plagiarism! Plot your stories around – not within! Having a car gave me more scope for my book-selling, I was meeting more people, because I was able to go straight home as soon as my quota was reached. In the little town of Royston, I met a customer who, had read of my exploits and wanted to follow suit, but not in the book line – it was painting!

He showed me his water-colours, his sketches, and even a portrait. I thought they were very good, and asked him why they weren't bringing him in a lucrative living. He seemed a rather shy, modest man, who wasn't aware of his talent.

"I've had one or two exhibitions, but only sold a few. The chap at the 'Rose and Crown' allows me to hang a few permanently around the walls, but, it doesn't amount to much, and they get soiled through people touching them!

It seemed to me the old, old, story. England isn't the best place to explore and nurture talent, it was fast becoming a do-it-yourself nation. The artist, must have read my thoughts.

"Give me the low down on selling, I'm having a go myself, but, the thought of knocking at my first door, frightens me to death!"

Studying his face, I felt he had a good "head"

start. It was honest, fresh, with lovely blue eyes, from under shaggy sandy coloured eye-brows. I thought of my first knock at the door! I tried hard to give him the benefit of my years of experience. You must have complete faith in what you are selling, *you* know it's good, but the customer doesn't, so you must make him believe that you have a commodity that he wants. Don't knock at the door, too hard, but, just hard enough to be heard. A loud insistant knock, sounds too impatient, too arrogant, and maybe the resident will be anti-sales before she even sets eyes on the salesman.

Should there be a bell as well as a knocker, use the bell first, it has a deeper penetration for a customer at the back of the house. Listen for the bell actually ringing, if you're not sure of its functioning then reinforce your call with a knock.

Don't have a set form of patter, play it by ear, until you see who it is coming to meet you. A breezy Colonel type character, wouldn't lend itself to a smarmy dollop of sales talk. In this case, you would have to be bright, quick to the point – and away!

The customer has quite a few tell-tale mannerisms which give a clue to the likelihood of the sale. The door will be gently pushed to a close during sales talk, only slightly mind you, but it's there to see, so a little more effort to break through her barrier. Mark you, I said effort – not pressure!

The face can be a false clue, I have sold many times, to a person with a grim, determined "No Sale" look. But, remember, times are changing, muggings, bodily attacks are prevalent. It's possible that the woman uses her face as a kind of security against anyone harming her.

Another nice sign, is when she reaches across to the hall stand to get her handbag.

Author writing by the tent

Taking the book from you, peeping in, then holding the closed book to her body, is a sure sign of a sale. This is her book! It's a psychological point in many cases that as soon as the customer handles the book, the more likely a sale will develop.

Talk in a confident manner, a nice familiar tone, not hurried in any way. In the case of the picture to be sold, "I think this would look nice in your hall!" would be a nice opening gesture.

Now back to books. Don't flatter. Don't in any, way be personal. Don't gossip about *her* next door. Should you be selling to a home with children, push home your view that nowadays kiddies should get a choice on what they read. Mothers, I'm afraid, get conned very easily when it concerns their kiddies. They fall for the photo-competition, the Education officers agreeing that the type of book you're selling, is a must for her child.

Now for the time wasting customer, who, doesn't intend to buy, merely, to pass a little time before "hubby gets home for dinner". Usually, she folds her arms, leans forward, and agrees with everything you say. "Isn't it lovely!" "Ooh, it's cheap isn't it", "How ever do you manage to write, wish I could, my teacher said I was very good at composition!" Nine times out of ten, they end up with. "Well, give me a call next time you're round – I'll have to go now, hubby'll be home soon!"

You *must* accept the fact that no-one *need* buy, so don't get too worried about the odd "No". The law of averages is on your side, and ask yourself "Do *I* buy at the door every time?"

Dangers at the door. Watch how you describe your book, price, details, never ever adopt the foot-in-the-door attitude. I've read letters to Editors, bemoaning the fact that door-to-door salesmen ever exist. Some people have a built in prejudice against *anyone* calling at the door.

Without my glasses, I'm not too hot at reading small print. After knocking a door the irate lady pointed to a small sign at the side of the door. "No Canvassers. No Circulars".

I apologised profusely pointing out that I hadn't noticed the sign. To my surprise she showed a marked interest in my book, ending up buying a couple of volumes. But a case like hers, I'm sure, is a "one off!"

The main feature of door-to-door selling is honesty! You *must* direct your sales talk, to the fact that you *will* be seeing the customer again. Most bad reports concerning door-to-door selling come from "High Pressure" salesmen who work on commission only, and sweep through a town like a swam of locusts, never to be seen in the vicinity again. If you've got something *good* to sell, and people try it once, they'll buy again. I've proved it time after time. Remember, the shop's record, according to T.V. programmes, aren't all that good! *They*, at times sell shoddy goods. But a good door-to-doorman doesn't. I told the would-be-salesman to adapt what I had told him, to picture selling, and I was sure he'd succeed!

CHAPTER 13

Doorstep Hiccups

Following on the heels of my teaching session to the young artist, on selling his creations at the door, comes an account of the things that can go wrong on the doorstep. I was working in a part of Cambridge, which was a little notorious for its mugging and conning activities.

My stint was nearly finished, I had just four books to sell, to finish my quota for the day. Accidently, I caught the pocket of my raincoat on a protruding latch on a gate, giving it a rather unsightly tear.

As it was raining, I decided to keep the coat on, which, I agree, to a patrolling very young policeman on the opposite side of the street, could look suspicious. The four books seemed to have taken ages to get disposed of, but, I was at last free to meet a steely-eyed copper at the corner of the street, where he had stalked me.

"You got a licence?" he rapped out. Years back in my brush selling days I had what was then known as a Peddler's Licence, it cost me one shilling, and as far as I remember it lasted your lifetime.

I felt real stupid as I put this point to the copper, who was rocking backwards and forward on his heels, true P.C. 49 fashion.

"Have to look into this! Name and address? Oh, and I'd advise you not to do any more selling door-to-door, until you hear from us – get me?"

On the way home, I got to reckoning. It was quite possible, that my name could stay on their files for donkey's years, before they got round to looking at it. I had three thousand books left of my 5,000 run-off. I'd never sell them! So I decided on going round the police station myself, and sort out the matter.

If the young copper had seen it, he would have blushed a deep red. Approaching the reception desk, I could see four policemen in shirt sleeves working away at their typewriters. Spotting me, one of them shouted across, "Oh, Mr Unwin, my missus wants your latest book, you will be popping round again this year, won't you? You know the address, 147 Coleridge Road!"

Two of the other constables after a whispered conversation with the one who had placed in his order, both shouted across "Give us a look in too, won't you. We enjoyed your last book about the Army!"

Smiling, the reception duty copper attended to my request on how the law stands regarding door-to-door selling, and the licence thereof. Opening an enormous tome he waded through its dusty pages, "Now, let me see, wet fish, fresh fruit, perishable goods act, can't see anything yet, Mr Unwin. Oh, by the way, you produce your own work, sort of creative labours, I think it comes under. No, Mr Unwin, you need no peddlers' licence to sell a work of art of your own creation. O.K., boy!"

As he finished, he looked across to his fellow workers, then back again at me. "By the way, where were you working when the constable stopped you, and can you describe him to me." I did my best as charitably as possible. My reply brought guffaws of laughter, and the remark "Oh, it's him again, eh!"

I dare say, since then, at least, I hope so, the young copper has made many more illustrious catches, than me. I suppose to him, I was the one that got away!

Another rumpus at the door, came about through my selling brushes to a customer's mother. The customer, then, a little girl, had received from me, what we termed sample gifts, in the shape of a small tin of polish which kiddies loved to polish their dollshouses with. Now, years later, as a bookseller, I was again at her door. To heighten the pleasure at seeing me, she told me that I'd mentioned her mother in one of my books, since then, her mother had passed away.

Over a cup of tea, we were discussing what a lovable person her mother had been, when in walked her husband. Just before his entry, while he was putting his cycle in the shed, the customer's little girl had said something which caused us to laugh out loud. I think this had set, an already paranoid mind, over the threshold of tolerance level, to, well above it. The man literally exploded, "So this is how you hatch your plots is it. Galivanting around with another man's wife. No wonder, you manage a book a year, plenty of material, eh, never run short do you?"

With my nursing experience behind me, I knew it would be fatal to attempt to argue with the man. Instead, I looked across to his wife. "You tell him. Tell him I've known you since you were a child – !"

The man made a lunge at me, which, I easily avoided, as, he was blind with rage. Without more ado, I made for the door, realising that discretion was the better part of valour. Luckily, the man thought he'd done enough in chasing me away, and didn't bother to follow, maybe, the frightened child, and screaming wife, might have set the neighbours talking.

A few doors down, I was told about the husband's paranoid antics. The wife had gone "home to mother" several times before her mum's death. It was just one of those things, of all the thousands of homes I visit, there's bound to be a "one off" occurrance.

Animals too, can be a little time consuming. Usually, I get on well with them. Never run away, stand your ground, talk in a soft voice, never put out your hand to stroke them, this, they feel is an act of aggression.

Sometimes, I smile at the way a few clients, come to the door, with a snarling, snapping ferocious dog, as, they seem to be pulling it back with little regard for the dog's half strangled throat. I'd love to say to them "Is this the way you greet your best friend, or the Vicar!"

In these days of muggings, I suppose it's another way of saying, "No, keep away!"

One day, a man came to the door to greet me, he was pulling at a big black dog, which, seemed prepared to tear me to bits. I spoke to the dog softly, the dog seemed to understand that I wasn't his enemy, and allowed me to give him a quick pat on the head. Its owner was so furious at my having broken the dog's snarling attitude, that, he gave the dog an extra pull on its throat – the dog, promptly bit him!

It would have been much easier for the man to have left his dog in the kitchen, and said a polite "No" at the door.

Now we come to the "never buy at the door" brigade! I can understand their reason, it's their decision, and it saves me time, as I'm able to quickly get to the next sale, instead, of perhaps wasting time on a "No Sale!"

But, some people do it in a very arrogant way. For these, I have a little story, which, funnily enough, is quite true. I tell them about us, a newly married couple, feeling sorry for some gypsies at our door, selling clothes pegs, we purchased three-dozen for about 1/-.

Today, most of those pegs are still in use, the ones we had to buy at the shop, to supplement the others, at the birth of our two children, have long since gone. I tell them that the newspring pegs, break far too easily – not a patch on the gypsies' which we bought at the door – I told them at times, a bargain can be had at the doorstep.

It's never made a sale, but gives the dogmatic person, food for thought.

Back to animals again, a little black dog used to meet me at the beginning of my round on a busy estate. It followed me from door to door, sitting patiently at the gate, then moving onto the next house. At the end of my round, it would toddle off home. A tame pigeon, sitting on a fence, at my appearance, it would flap on to my shoulder, then allow me to carry it around for quite a while.

One dog, would arrive on the doorstep just as its owner did. It would sit placidly while we conducted our sales talk. At the end of which, it would walk slowly behind me to the gate. Just as I was about to open the gate, it would make a quick grab at my ankles, mostly getting in every time. I never let on to the lady about this, which, had been going on for several years.

One evening, I saw a snippet in the local rag. A postman had taken to court a woman for not keeping her dog under control. Apparently, more than once it had savagely bitten him. To my surprise, it gave the address of my little heel-snapper. The magistrate ordered the dog to be destroyed. The dog, must have played the same trick on the postman, as it did on me. The next time I saw the woman, her first words were, "You've heard about my poor little dog, haven't you, wouldn't hurt a fly, my little chap!"

I couldn't resist telling the truth, I thought maybe she'd buy another dog. You do have to think about the poor old postman – after all, didn't he once bring me my coveted slim envelope, and plop in on to my mat?

Another little hiccup for door-to-door salesmen, is the telephone. In the middle of the sales "run-up", it rings. The householder, runs off, leaving you on the doorstep. Some are wonderful, I've known them, after preliminary introductions, to say "Will you ring back, I've a gentleman at the door". Of course, you can't expect everyone to be in the same mould, after all the P.O. does say "Make someone happy, give them a ring!"

Mind you, it does give a householder a good reason to get rid of an unwelcome high-pressure sales man, "Sorry, I'm on the phone!"

Children, sometimes, can be good unwitting sale killers. Clicking the letter-box, quite loudly, is a ploy adopted by many. Trying to close the door, and pleading "Can I have one, Mummy?" often kills a sale.

Fighting, coming from the back kitchen, the cries and screams, are enough to send the harrassed housewife running from the front door, children seem to time their *squabbling* to the advent of the sales folk.

Husbands, can, at times, be a major hiccup. Bless their hearts, as man of the house, they are out to show their supremacy. And, doesn't the wicked door-to-door man "con" their pretty little wives, while they are out at work, leaving her defenceless.

So they arrive at the door, grim faced, and give short shrift to the unlucky salesman.

Before I go any further, all these hiccups are in the minority, as I've said before, most people I meet, are marvellous. I've found over the years, in my many thousands of calls at the door, that people *are* wonderful. If you are honest, they know you, and they want what you are selling – they're great. I've been paid in small coins, taken from the telephone savings box. I've had mums with knives sliding out coins from unused money boxes. They take from the milkman's money, from the rent money (they put it back, later). Small children have "lent" mum money from their Christmas boxes, you may depend on their getting good interest from mum!

'PC 49' stopping Unwin in street

One dear old lady, she always bought a book each year from me. On that particular day, she couldn't "find a bean", so I left the book with her, on the stipulation that she mustn't worry, she could pay me next time round.

At least two hours later, from the opposite side of the street, I saw the dear old soul waiting at her gate. She had borrowed the money from her neighbour, and had been waiting for me to come down on the other side of the street.

A store of wealth in human stories can be had from going round homes, year in, and year out!

Including my brush selling days, my milk round, my colporteurs days, I've been calling round houses for the last forty years.

"That's the same old man, who, used to call on mum!" the young newly wed would say.

A child, answering the door, to mum's shout from the kitchen, "Who is it?" usually replies, "It's that old man, again, selling books, mum!"

I've had to call at the doctor's for housebound people, to send him scurrying round, because they've had a stroke, or been taken ill during the night.

I've feared for very young children, who, in night attire, came to the door at night, while the parents are watching T.V. A demanding "who is it, Janet?" doesn't make up for the danger involved. For all they know, I could take the child away.

I counter this, with a very loud "Oh, you are a brave little girl, coming to the door at night!"

This ploy, usually works with a red faced mum fetching in her would-be maid.

Sometimes, I put myself in their position. A miserable day, news on T.V. gloomy. Hubby been made redundant, illness in the house. A knock at the door, just as they were in the middle of washing up, there's me, with a £2 book for sale. And still they smile, "Oh, I enjoyed your last book, lent it to my daughter in America, she used to live here you know, I miss her. Yes, I must get your latest, would you like a cup of tea?"

I don't know how *I* would re-act in like circumstances!

Another thing, the media, get the public all wrong at times. Going round the next day, after the press have "gone to town" on some political issue, I find they rarely remember the subject, most distrust politicians, they've been let down so many times with promises, and last minute "goodies" offered before an election, whereas, they have had to put up with years of this government!

Take a burly lorry driver with a tabloid. He reads the back page for sports news, inside for racing form, absorbs any pin-ups going. The editor who has strung together a load of biased, one way tripe, against whoever is the opposition, would get a shock to realise that the dear old lorry driver, either hasn't read a word of it. If he has, he doesn't believe a word of it, or, is more concerned to see if he's won anything on Bingo, or catch up with the latest film-star gossip columns – this, of course, he believes more readily than the political issues.

People, I find, store much of their desires on the fortnight holiday, which, for the whole year, they've scrimped and saved for. They, go round to the big stores to clothe their young hopefuls on their first day at school. They attend Speech Days, Carol Services, and at Christmas, watch they tiny tots bravely take over the role of Baby Jesus in the awaited Nativity play.

Mind you, they have their little moans on the bus. I heard one woman remark to another, her neighbour, Mr Kelly had just been elected as councillor for a tiny ward in that area.

"I see Mr Kelly's got in then! Now, we should see the Country get a little better off!" came the reply.

My sales at the door, were soaring beyond my initial dreams. A telephone call from a Mr Anthony Lee, reputedly from Thames Television, got to my ego again.

He'd heard about my selling exploits and would like to do a programme on me, I think it was called "After Four" and usually dealt with "one-off" exploits. Mr Lee asked me many questions, and ended up with promising to call on me.

Six months went by, I'd almost forgotten the incident, then he rang again.

"Still pounding the beat, Mr Unwin?" were his first words. I filled in all the missing details since his last call. Once again, he promised to call on me, even to the extent of asking me for a detailed means of getting to my home.

But, nothing came of it, I sometimes think he was a practical joker – but it did me no harm, other than denting that terrible ego, again!

CHAPTER 14

"Scoop" Wilson

I met "Scoop" Wilson one drizzly morning, he was fetching in his half-pint bottle of milk. "What are you selling, boy, looks to me, you could do with a cup of tea?"

Taking him up on this, I entered the small kitchen of his council flat. Putting on the kettle, he ushered me into his front room. The room was dusty, so dusty, that he couldn't possibly have kept a bird – it would have died of psittacosis! On a large table stood an old fashioned typewriter, it looked like a small engine. Scattered around the table were reference books, all kinds of Journals, "Spectator", "Listener", "Horse and Hound", on almost every chair were old newspapers. A large nail, driven into the wall, had, stuck through it, yellow cuttings of news snippets. At the side of the typewriter, stood a faded looking copy of Roget's Thesaurus.

With the tea under way, I had just about caught my breath, as my host looked across to me, holding out a welcoming hand, he said "Scoop" Wilson at your service. "Scoop", had character written all over him. He was a cross between Schnozzle

Durante and Mr Magoo, the cartoon character!

"I suppose you've guessed – I'm a journalist, free-lance, you might say. What's that your selling?"

Handing him a copy of "Gentle Tales of Old Cambridge", I studied him further, as he flicked over the pages of my book.

His nose, cherry red, was of major proportion, small twinkling eyes, set well back into his head. Wickedly, I thought of his nickname, "Scoop", he certainly had a good nose for news!

"You've got a racy kind of style, sort of casual like, people like your smooth writing, weren't like that in the old days, you wouldn't have got away with it, a few ain'ts, and wotchers, and you'd be out on your ear!"

I smiled back on the old man, I guessed he must have been around the seventy mark.

"Any tips for a budding young writer?" I asked.

"Keep your nose to the ground boy. Always carry a note book with you, as soon as a thought comes into your head – get it down. In my early days, I used to wake up in the morning with a hellava idea, like a fool I didn't jot it down. Then weeks later, I'd see it in the papers, someone else had got in first!"

I suppose journalism is a bit of a rat-race isn't it?" I asked.

"Scoop" poured out another cup of tea. "You get them in all sorts of ways. Do you know boy, I used to write a little Christmas story, for a local paper, back in Newcastle this was. Each year they printed it, I'm sure the kids loved it. One of the big-wigs of the paper, used to write, what he called the Monday Column, a bits and pieces affair, quite good, really. In one article, he was pulling Al Jolson to bits, said he was third-rate, and never a real entertainer! I took him to task on this, wrote in a letter to the Editor, you know the stuff, I sort of championed old Al – !"

"What happened?" I broke, in to give "Scoop" a break, as he'd managed it all in one breath.

"Well, I never got another Christmas Story in the paper, I reckon this fellow took it out on me by sort of blacklisting my stuff, that's life boy!"

Looking round "Scoop's" room, I could see no sign of a woman's hand.

"You never married, then, "Scoop"?" I ventured.

The old journalist smiled, "You know boy, writing, don't lend itself to the feminine touch. Used to have a housekeeper, live in, you know the racket, always bringing in cups of coffee, just as I was in the middle of a nice little purple passage. I must have wasted hours drinking coffee I didn't want. Next thing, it was the curtains, up and down like a yo-yo. Look at them now, too dirty for anyone to look in, and just about clean enough for me to look out!"

"What about, money, "Scoop" – how do you manage?"

"I'm always sending out something. Newspapers all over the U.K., take my stuff. So, every week or so, a little money comes my way. I've even tried my hand at the women's papers. You know, boy, little bits of advice on this, and that, funny little experiences, and all that. A tenner a throw nowadays, you know, boy, there's a certain woman who writes in all the journals, signs herself in a slightly different way, but sends the same story to different magazines. They copped her out one day, and put a nice little note that their paper wouldn't print stale news features!"

Picking up the used cups, I took them into the kitchen, placing them in the sink. I could hear the patter of the rain on the window, my quota was almost completed, just one more book to sell. I reckoned that I could afford to spend a little more time with the old writer.

Noticing a sheet of paper clamped between the metal jaws of his typewriter, I queried on what "Scoop" was up to next.

"A little documentary on the changes that I've seen, since I came here fifty years ago!" "Scoop" gave me a detailed account: in those days everything was spanking new, nice creosoted fences around the gardens. People came in from the slums around the centre of the City. Used to paying 1/6d or 2/- rent, they found the extra Council rents a little too much. Unemployment was a cancer eating into their very being. Things got so bad, that the fences around the gardens were used for firewood. In one case, a tenant even chopped up a door in order to obtain firewood. The "never, never" boys were having a field day, debts grew, as tired mother tried to clothe their kids in a decent manner.

Prostitution was no stranger to the area, thieving from their own kind was the done thing. Where, once, the back door was always open, now doors were locked, anyone, lucky to bring home a pay packet would have to watch out for the Friday night "visitor".

"Things look a little better now, "Scoop?" I was taking in the new fencing, the fresh paint, the steel framed windows, in the garden were new baths, waiting to be installed.

"Scoop" nodded. "The newly elected Council got cracking. Tenants' associations were formed, committees on this, that, and the other, made their own rules. There's a house up the road, with a large sign outside the front gate. It tells you which house is being used for toddler groups, baby sitting, parental problems. The telephone numbers of various people willing to assist on these projects were listed. Jumble sales, Christmas Fayre, anything to collect enough cash to fund a pensioners' outing, or, a kiddies' trip to the seaside, were in progress – I guess you could say, things have improved-and, remember, unemployment in this area is still a problem!"

"Where will you sell the article?"

"To an upmarket paper. You know the sort, "Riding to Hounds", "Fortnum & Mason", Harrods, all come second nature to its readers, a little bit of "Pygmalion" thrown in with the caviare. They don't know these places exist, just as our neighbours around here are oblivious to their way of life – it's news, it's journalism, you have to keep a sharp eye out, boy!"

What do you, really, as a professional writer, think of my taking on what I've so far achieved?"

"Scoop" put the kettle on, then returned to the front room.

"I've followed you from the start. I know all about the vanity author lark, and the vanity publishers, too. You did the right thing boy. Getting anything published today is nigh impossible. I don't blame the poor old publishers, it costs so much to launch a book, you daren't take chances. I've written little booklets on travel, about the city's tourists attractions, but, somehow, I can't make the grade with a novel. Six times I've sent it out, each time the dreaded rejection-slip, gets pushed through the letter-box!"

"Ever tried a Writer's Circle, or, haven't you got a writing group around here?" I asked.

"Scoop" smiled, "Well, one day I swallowed my pride, and joined. A nice little group, just one male, in a circle of thirty. Maybe, I thought, someone might just have enough connections to put me on to a publisher. Each week we'd meet, and read out our little masterpieces. It was the old, old, story, the converted preaching, to the converted, no real bite, no solid constructive criticism. Bless their hearts, they all meant well. The other male was writing a novel, each week he'd read out an excerpt.

Somehow, he was obsessed with sex. Every paragraph, dealt with his hero's activities with the opposite sex. It seemed that in his mind, the only way to make it in the literary world, was through the eyes of a Harold Robbins type of literature. The dear ladies listened intently, not a blush to be seen (a writer has to be broadminded) at the end, "It's coming along nicely, Reginald!" "Perhaps the dialogue is a little stilted!" These asides were Reginald's reward, for what was, undoubtedly," a hard night's work".

"Scoop" poured out yet, another cup of tea. "Once a month a guest speaker would come along.

An editor of a glossy womans' journal, or, an expert on hairdressing, with a view to the circle sending in a list of what they expect from the modern day salon. All very nice, the editor would toss out some interesting hints, but none, other than the old chestnut's rule, of margins, copyright, presentation, markets, but, never a real attempt to teach the elusive art of writing a novel!"

"Scoop" signed. "Soon as I found myself on the rota for washing up the tea-cups, I called it a day. I don't like to criticise a writing circle. Many people find it a haven against loneliness, should they manage an acceptance of their manuscript, well, what a bonus! And, there *were* acceptances: but, on the whole, I often wonder how lovely it would be, if, one was at college for three years on a writing course. Just imagine being able to call the attention of a Writer Tutor to your latest brainchild, being advised on where to send it, and able to see him again, and again, until you got it right. After all, a Tutor is judged against his failures!"

"Scoop", from a tin box on the window-sill, took out £2 in silver, handing it to me, he said "There, boy, I'll buy your book, you might say it's "Coals to Newcastle", but, a good writer gets his stories from all sources!"

I couldn't but help liking "Scoop". He was so natural, not for him the hoity-toity attitude that some writers take. I remember going to the Bookman's Club, a second time. The group present, seem to "suss" out a member, find out if his credentials are up to their "standard". Should they be so, then, they would hob-nob with him, on the strength that it's good to be seen in the company of that person. Anyone else, gets a plastic smile!

Looking over "Scoop", I asked, a little tongue in cheek, "When are you likely to call it a day?"

"I pay in a Literary Club's pension scheme. Should I get a bit low on material, cop for an illness, which prevents me writing for a living, well, then I'll pack it in!"

As he spoke, a figure passed the window. "Scoop", although I hadn't noticed, was on to it, in a flash!

"You know, boy, I never need go short of material around here. That fellow, passing by, looks a typical dirty old man brigade. You'd never believe it, but, he was allowed to rent a Church hall on the pretext of running a teenage dance group. *I* couldn't believe it, until I saw the 'ad' in the paper. "Tinkle Bell dance group to be formed. Auditions on Saturday next 2 p.m. until 5 p.m. Trained instructor available. Apply Church Hall, Biddington Road".

"And then?" I laughed in anticipation of his reply.

"Yes, you've guessed it! But, the crunch came, and that's where we writers get our themes from, when a friend of mine, who, runs jumble sales for charity, was unable to rent the hall, because the Vicar, "doesn't agree, with letting out the hall, for anything other, than his *own* Church's fund raising!"

It was getting late, but the rain had stopped. With "Scoop" having bought my quota copy, I was in no real hurry to leave the old fellow. Sensing this, he showed me around his book shelves, and opened up the dusty files he had strewn around his|desk. "Never throw away old copy. Stuff you've had rejected in your early days, can be brought to the light, dusted up, and sent out again. I've written short stories, maybe with a little too much imagination, which, after a few years, the "Well's" type of story has come true, the things which, then, seemed outrageous, now are regarded common-place. Do you know, boy, *I* invented the then unheard of "Go-Kart". In a story of a young boy, I had his father make him a box-on-wheels. The doting dad, pushing the new contraption downhill with his son, a proud passenger, named it, unwittingly, "Go-Kart", mainly because it went."

I had to take my leave of the journalist, cum-author, cum-philosopher. One day, I'm sure, I'll write a story about "Scoop". He'd been a great inspiration to me, even to the extent of knowing, at seventy, I could still be churning stuff out like the old masters – by then, maybe, I'd be a little nearer his class.

Walking back to my car, through the maze of passage ways, and plethora of cul-de-sacs, I thought of the wonderful store of stories, which, come out of the setting. I remembered the tips I'd received from the Writers Ring, as passing a small private homes estate tucked away amidst the Council homes, I saw a magnificent new house, with a large sign "Show House".

At one time, the house had just been a structure of bricks and mortar. Now, it stood resplendent with posh curtains, shining windows, de-luxe

'Scoop' Wilson

furniture, gleaming working tops and a kitchen for making cooking a pleasure instead of a chore. I thought what a lovely lesson for the beginner writer. He must learn that a story from its original plot, must go to the finished touch. Many of my failures came almost because all I had to offer was a skeleton of bricks and mortar. In those days I thought it quite enough until meeting people like "Scoop".

One, or, two, homes with baths, once standing in the front garden, were now sitting snugly in their new bathrooms. The old wives' tale of coal being stored in the bath, was now regarded as a myth. As "Scoop" had pointed out, many changes had been wrought, families, in their new setting, were walking tall!

A great new foundation for story lines, I thought, poor old "Scoop" wouldn't live to see it all. But why should Dallas, Dynasty and Coronation Street monopolise the screen, when real life, and real people were here for the taking!

CHAPTER 15

Jenny's Hospitalisation

Jenny's arthritis had taken a turn for the worse. The two operations on her knees were not satisfactory. The patella, a protection around the knee-joint, had not fallen into place, so a second operation on that particular knee, had to be done. The arthritis "flare-ups" were getting more prevalent, so it was decided upon Jenny's admittance to hospital.

The convalescent hospital chosen, was that of a place near North Walsham, well out in the sticks. This meant, a long journey, three times a week for me, but, as Jenny had been such a power-horse of encouragement for my taking up writing, I, was only too pleased to give her a little of *my* time. There is little doubt that arthritis is a very crippling disease, and, I'm afraid, that unless you suffer yourself, you are not likely to understand the suffering of others!

In films, or stories, the rheumatic sufferer, the lumbago pains undergone by hapless victims, are usually met with gales of laughter. My grandmother was a constant sufferer of such ailments. Sitting into a chair was almost a ritual with her, "ohs" and "ahs" with a final grunt of relief as she sank into an armchair that greeted her with open arms.

How many of us, have not laughed, at the sight of the old Colonel, sitting with his gouty foot bathed in thick bandages, and up comes the waiter, with drinks, to promptly drop something on the Colonel's foot.

Getting back to my grandmother, I paid dearly for laughing at her plight. Years after her death, as I was bending over to pick out a brush from my delivery basket, I experienced a most terrible pain in the middle of my back, I was unable to straighten up, a customer had to help me into her house, until the pain subsided – but, my immediate reaction, was to think back on my grandmother's suffering, and my laughing at her!

However, despite Jenny's time away from home, I was still storing up material for plots, themes, and anecdotes. Visiting her one day at the hospital, I was struck by the worried looks of many of the patients, who, at that time were all seated in the Common Room. Some were holding their necks on one side, others were sitting with collars turned up. On my arrival, Jenny, with her nursing experience behind her, had chosen a chair in a sensible position, she looked at me knowingly, and pointed to the windows.

It was a very cold day, the wind being gusty. The room was made cold, with the cold breeze playing on to the patients. Without more ado, I closed the windows, which, brought about a bout of clapping from the grateful patients. It turned out a vicious circle, because, the noise brought in an irate matron, who, immediately opened the windows. Without bothering to find out the culprit, she stormed out! I stepped up and closed them again!

'Paper peddlars'

Thinking it a better policy to confront the matron, rather than carry on a "your move" silly game, I went to her office. I told her that I had nursed elderly patients for at least ten years, of both sexes, and realised, that with their impaired circulation, they felt the cold more than the average younger person. As, I had experienced the sufferings of an arthritic person, i.e. my wife, it was even more imperative, that, they were not subjected to cold conditions. I fully understood that fresh air was a must, in regard to maintaining good health, but, fresh air, and cold draughts, were two different aspects in the quest for happy convalescence!

She seemed too dumbfounded to be able to make a positive reply, luckily, for her, the phone rang, which gave me an excuse not to embarrass her further.

True to human nature, my little foray, didn't help Jenny one iota, the rest of her stay at the hospital, was made less tolerable, through a spiteful matron. With Jenny back home, in better health, despite the little trauma, I settled back into my selling books and writing sessions.

To my surprise, in a little side-road off Shelford Road, I came across John Alexander, the News editor. He was about to take up a post in the Midlands, a kind of promotion really! The familiar "Sold" notice, stood outside his house, and the household were in the throes of packing their belongings.

Calling me in, John, shook hands with me, congratulating me on my successful writing since the Stockwell fiasco. "My daughter thoroughly enjoyed your latest book. The chapter about the Means Test man, especially. I reckon every child her age, should be *made* to read it, they don't know what life was like in those days!" (The News printed the whole chapter, in one of their feature Editorials)

So, once again,. the feud of the Stockwell story had come to its logical conclusion – look at both sides of the coin!

The Means Test man, was a person, of whom, as a very small child, I had heard poignant stories from poverty-stricken mothers. Rather than hand out an extra penny, to feed a family, the Government of the day, chose to make the victims of unemployment, sell off anything with a semblance of value, be it sentimental or, even a broken down radio. Ironically, the father concerned, would recently have spent years in the trenches of the First World War!

Activity in Market Hostel, had reached a crescendo, of strikes, demos, sit-ins, and a general aspect of anarchy. It was giving me a good deal of material for my book "In the Shadow of King's". Jenny was struggling gamely, with the job as Hostel Keeper, with my helping her as much as possible.

Of my rounds, I had decided to include St. Neots in my calls. With my car proving a grand asset, I was able to take in more ground, and thus increase readership. I found that after my visiting a new town, or village, letters of appreciation came in, with a request for more of my earlier books. On my first visit to St. Neots, I had an unusual experience.

Leaving Cambridge on a sunny morning in November, I was visualising a nice pleasant day selling. After passing the Papworth crossing, I noticed that conditions were quickly changing. Lorries coming from the opposite direction, were covered in a hoary frost-like substance, with snow, also in the mixture. It was changing to bitterly cold, as opposed to the early sunshine.

I just about made it to St. Neots, and pulled into a convenient lay-by on the edge of the town. A dense fog-like atmosphere came over the town, with a helping of icy snow for good measure.

Locking the car, I put on a top coat, and walked the short distance into St. Neots. Musing, on the way, the reason for the climatic change, all within half-an-hour, was the fact, that I was travelling further North.

In the centre of the shopping precinct, I was about to look in a book-store window with a view to placate my new book. Suddenly, the blast of a gun exploded into the quietness of the old market town. The shot, seemed to have come from the Woolworth store. A crowd began to gather, but, I decided that I would stay on the pavement, and watch proceedings. Police, ambulances, roared up to the scene, with harassed shop assistants leading the way into the store, and the scene of the shooting.

As I waited, the snow, fog and inclement weather, had gradually disappeared leaving a hazy sunshine in its place.

With true professionalism, I returned to the car, to start my selling. St. Neots town was a pretty little place, wide-spread and growing rapidly. As I went from house to house, a few housewives, asked me if I'd heard anything about the "Shooting", eventually, I got the full story. It appeared that a man burst into the store, mad with rage at the discovery of his wife's infidelity. No one seemed to know if the irate husband, had actually shot his wife, or, her lover, or, even if anyone had been killed!

Later, in a small street, I found a group of American airmen from the nearby aerodromes, who, had been housed in St. Neots. They were leaving England within a few months, my book, they regarded, as a nice memento of their stay in England!

But, to my delight, civilians too were interested in my book, ordinary housewives, who, once, had had connections with Cambridge. By lunch, I had sold my quota, and was on my way home.

I was very pleased with my day's work. It had proved to me, that people will buy books, as long as you explain what it's all about. St. Neots is a distance of twenty-five miles from Cambridge, which geographically might seem a long way to expect to sell a book, about Cambridge. But, I found many St. Neots residents, actually, worked in Cambridge.

Another point is how many people actually visit the bookshops in quest of books for themselves. Children, yes, dear old mums, are always poking about looking for something they read as small children. Tiger Tim, Rainbow, Comic Cuts, Funny Wonder all the fun laden periodicals that gave them so much pleasure. I well remember, three little characters, "Pip", "Squeak", and "Wilfred", they always ended their little sojourn with one of them saying "I am surprised!"

Passing Hardwick on my way home, I came across a startling revelation. Having passed a huge square mass of compressed paper standing on the grass verge, further down, I encountered a strange couple. They appeared to be gypsies, but, as man and woman, there seemed something different. Both were attending a large mass of paper similar to the one I had seen farther up the road. Stopping the car, I strode across to investigate, having in mind, that, from this, I might have a good theme for a story.

The couple were busily removing papers from the litter basket at the side of the road. These they folded up neatly, and, together with crushed paper cartons, they kind of moulded them all together, similar to the crushed car effect you see in scrap-yards. The finished creation wasn't yet as large as the previous one I'd passed, so to my amazement, the couple proceeded to half roll, and half push the giant mass of paper along to the next litter-cage at the nearby lay-by! During the operation the strange pair neither spoke, nor gave me a second glance. Getting back into the car, a little way down, I saw a Council worker cutting the side of a hedge. I called him over and asked if he knew anything about the odd couple.

Wiping his forehead, with the traditional red-spotted handkerchief, he put down his clippers "I reckon nobody knows much about them, mister. Seems they travel all over the country collecting paper, and like ants, they roll it along from town to town. They caused a hell of a do in St. Neots, held up the traffic something cruel, had to get the police, they did!"

I smiled at the man "I wonder why they do it. Are they collecting for charity, or, something?"

"No. I went to my doctor last night, got a little rash on me shoulder, he reckons it's sweat, but I tells him about it, I mean, about the paper rollers. He reckons they're what you call 'schitzy', or summat, the police ought to lock them up, he said!"

Carrying on my journey home, I got to thinking, how on earth, if they were schizophrenic, can one induce the other to carry out the same task. During my nursing career I had tended many schizophrenic patients, one case came to mind. Two old sisters had lived together for years. One, had been diagnosed as having a schizophrenic element. The other sister was perfectly normal. But, as the years of living together passed by, it was found they too, had a craze for collecting newspapers, they were stacked high in every room, under the bed, until for hygiene reasons the welfare department was informed.

The result of their investigation, made strange reading, because, from neighbours reports, it was evident that *both* sisters were engaged whole heartedly in the ridiculous pursuit of collecting paper. One sister had handed over, her schizophrenic trait to the other sister, at the expense of all logic. The place was filthy, mice ridden, neither sister had troubled to cook. They both were taken into care, put on to a special medication, and spent the rest of their days in a mental-hospital, with no further thought of newspaper collecting.

So, maybe, I thought, this could be the answer to our two heroic traffic stoppers. (Two weeks later, the police apprehended the pair as they caused a snarl-up in the City, confiscated the two mounds of newspaper, and, the couple were taken into custodial care into special Institutions.)

"Scoop" Wilson, I reasoned, would love to hear of my St. Neots, happening, so I called on him.

He was bent over his old faithful Remington, as I entered his flat. Over "Scoops" usual cuppa, I unfolded the strange story to him. "Good, lad!" he said, as I finished. "A good nose for a story, you're learning fast. Now, I'm going to get on my Phillips scooter, and take myself off to St. Neots. On the way, I hope to catch up with the paper-rollers, take a snap of them, then I'll go on, to get the low down on the shooting in St. Neots!"

"Could make a good story!" I replied. "Funny I should have come across it all in one day?"

"The couple are certainly getting into the '*papers*', laughed back Scoop.

"Scoop" put his cup down. "That's how it goes, boy. Weeks without nothin', – then wallop, it's all happening – but, I can't hang about, I'll have to get cracking – two stories in one day eh, thanks for coming boy!"

Back home to Jenny! As I mounted the stairs to our flat, I thought of a woman's lot. There's me out all day, with maybe Jenny sitting in pain, awaiting my return. Then I compromised a little, I couldn't really sit there, just watching her in pain, or do anything, bless her, she would say, "Now don't worry about me, I have plenty to take my mind off pain. It's the nights that are the worst.

Thank goodness, you're always at home at night!"

I comforted myself – it was true! A cup of tea brought to her chair as she watched telly, a goodnight kiss. (Well husbands do, don't they?) Then a cup of tea, first thing in the morning!

Jenny was in a good frame of mind. Mr. Murley had put her on to a new tablet "Brufen", it was proving a good antidote for arthritis pains!

"He considers me as his prize patient!" Jenny said proudly, "Reckons I'm marvellous, managing all these stairs, putting up with noisy students, and bickering bedmakers!"

As I sat close to Jenny, I told her of my day's happenings, of dear old "Scoop" Wilson, and watched her reactions. She was just as interested in what had happened to me, as I was about her day.

It dawned on me that sharing these things together, helped us both immensely. Going out in the cold, foggy, rainy mornings with the thought of an understanding wife behind me, made selling much more enjoyable; I couldn't present a smiling face at 8.30 a.m., without, as they say, "a good woman behind every successful man".

Then too, it helped when I was writing, knowing that through Jenny's back-up I had so far, sold approaching, 50,000 books. Maybe, I wasn't earning a fortune, but, I was putting a little bit of pleasure into homes. Even Jenny, in her role as hostel-keeper often gave advice to lonely first term students. Many times on returning home, I would find a student sitting at the table over a cup of tea, or coffee, having dried her eyes, was now heeding the advice of Jenny, that "First-term problems would be soon overcome – just teething problems, really" (King's was the first college to go co-ed)

And so it was, the day ended. I wondered how "Scoop" had fared with his journalistic jaunt to St. Neots.

The old Phillips scooter of his, was no joy ride, but business before pleasure, old "Scoop" would reason, the story line, would outweigh the bumps.

I reckoned, that if ever I came into a lot of money, I'd buy old "Scoop" a new car. Now that would make a nice story ending!

CHAPTER 16

A Talk on Mental Illness

Following the St. Neots adventure, as I returned from a day's selling, I found a young student waiting at the hostel. He told me that he wanted to go on in further studies, to become a psychiatrist. He asked me if I could help in any way, as apart from his ambitions in the mental field, he was doing an important thesis on psychology. He knew that I had been a psychiatric nurse, and was now a successful author.

When an older man, meets a young man, bent on bettering himself, seeking advice, it does something to him. Just as "Scoop" Wilson, must have been taken back to his early struggles, when giving me a few tips on writing. Thus, it was, with this young man, I *wanted* to help him, I felt I owed it him, as I had been through all the gambit of mental nursing, attended lectures, and studied all aspects of psychiatry. Psychiatry, by the way, is the practical application of psychology.

The student, Ronald, asked me to describe a patient's symptoms, suffering from paranoid schizophrenia. I cited a case. As a student nurse, I was on duty, when a man of about thirty, was brought in as an overnight-stay patient. The idea being, that he would be assessed on his mental condition, in order to allow his entering a half-way house, prior, to his ultimate discharge.

My task, was to see him bathed, and prepared for a full examination, both physically, and mentally. His name was Manning.

During the course of my nursing duty, I found him most amicable, talkative, and seemingly in full control of his mental faculties.

The conversation centred around sport, during which, Mr. Manning, showed great interest in cricket, Compton, Cowdrey, and Trueman, being among his favourites. With the examination trolley in position, I went off to inform the duty doctor of Mr. Manning's readiness for the assessment to take place.

"What's he like Nurse Unwin?" asked the duty Doctor, as with stethoscope at the ready, he was about to leave the clinic. I detected a slight twinkle in his eye as he made the question.

"He seems perfectly normal, to me. He knows all the sporting fraternity, and reckons that Tottenham Hotspurs will win the league this year!" I replied, confidently.

As we neared Mr. Manning's bedside, the doctor whispered to me "Now, take notice. This is all part of your training."

To my surprise, the doctor went through everything I'd done. Cricket, boxing, football, at which the patient didn't let me down in anyway, showing the same enthusiasm, as with myself. Suddenly, it happened, completely out of the blue!

The doctor stood back, and beckoned me to go to

the otherside of the bed. "Now, Mr. Manning, how do you get on with the vicar of your village, Mr. Runciman, I believe, his name?"

Mr. Manning went completely berserk, almost foaming at the mouth. Foul language, obscene oaths, he struggled to get out of bed, the bed was almost moving down the ward, as the doctor and I, tried to calm him.

George Pope

Eventually, with the coming of the charge nurse and a couple of nurses, the patient was given a Largactil injection, and put to bed in a side ward.

Back in the safety of the clinic, the Doctor explained. "I'd studied his case-notes before the examination. Something, I suggest, you, as a nurse, for safety's sake, should always do. From his notes, I knew that he was a dangerous paranoid, once the reason for his paranoi was touched upon, it acted as a catylistic fuse. Should the object of his paranoi have been in close proximity, well, I pity the poor old Vicar of his parish, he would undoubtedly have killed him."

Ronald, looked up from his notes. "Thank you, Mr. Unwin, I couldn't have wished for a better illustration. Could you enlighten me on the ordinary type of schizophrenia, not necessarily paranoia?"

My mind went back to the case-notes which I had studied when on night duty in the refractory ward. This patient, a man of only twenty-eight years, was an only son. His father had died, leaving him with his mother of some advanced years, to run the household. Albert, was a devoted son, he dusted, and polished, never went out at night, or week-ends. Indeed, Albert had been thoroughly spoiled by his mother since a small child.

The family were a religious unit, with the mother keeping a little crucifix in a prominent position on her mantel-piece. One day, during a bout of dusting, Albert knocked over the Crucifix on the fender, breaking off a hand of the figure of Christ.

From that moment, Albert developed a guilt complex, to such an extent, that it landed him into a psychiatric hospital. One day, Albert was inside a washing cubicle which houses an electric-shaving unit. The patient in the next cubicle, noticed the shaver had been buzzing away for a considerable time, then suddenly he saw blood oozing from the bottom of the door.

Calling a nurse, it was discovered, that Albert, under the noise of the electric shaver, had been sawing off his right hand with a bread knife, stolen from his ward kitchen. The gruesome discovery, brought out the basic elements of the true schizophrenic. Albert had obeyed the biblical statement of "an eye for an eye, a tooth for a tooth". He had stated that voices had told him to do what he had done.

I pointed out to Ronald, that *all* mental illness, is really no more than a prolongation of the very things that, we, as judged "normals", really do!

Say, for instance we go to a party which, turns out to be an utter disaster. On the way home, we mutter to ourselves "I shan't go to another of *his* parties!" To the patient, this, is the "voice". The difference is, that the poor mentally ill chappie, goes over the top. He cannot differentiate between the two, coupled with the guilt complex, which, again, the normal person on breaking the hand from the Crucifix momentarily, might feel guilty, but, would plan immediately to buy his mother another Crucifix. But, Albert, in his poor crazed mind, feels guilty to God; he can repay his "crime" by the only possible way "an eye for an eye, a tooth for a tooth" – in his case, "a hand for a hand".

Ronald had taken it all down in short-hand, something I wished I'd learned. It would have saved me a lot of work, had I studied the craft of shorthand.

The young student was very pleased with his miniature lecture. "I suppose taking notice of everything has helped your writing, you have always something to fall back on."

I realised how true this was. Many times, when writing a story, sometimes, with no set plan, other than the structure of the story, I've been able to put curtains up at the windows, carpet the floors, with little incidents, that flash into your mind. They come from no-where, but as psychology tells us, they belong to the "old brain", which is why elderly people remember more of the past, than of the present. The new brain, "the current file", is more easily forgotten!

Ronald's next request was for a case of "Catatonic schizophrenia," this very strange illness. There are many books covering all types of mental illness, written by, in some cases, authors' who have never actually nursed this type of patient. I can of course, relate only to the ones I nursed.

Michael Frost, was really a hypo-maniac, who, having gone through a terrible furore of the "mania" side of the malady, was now in a deep depression. The depression leads to an Anorexia Nervosa style of illness, where-by, the patients refuses to eat. The catatonic phase, is when the patient presents a kind of waxy posture, similar to the game we played as children called "Statues", when, we are "thrown" away from the lead player, and have to adopt a posture as that of a living statue. The best pose, wins the game!

The nurse has to carry out basic nursing, as that afforded a small baby. As you pick up a limb to wash, after washing, it drops, back to its original position.

This condition can last for a very long time. In the case of Michael, at least a month. I tried everything I could. Basically, he was a lovable simple country boy, I'd had an excellent relationship with him. I used to whisper in his ear, choose the type of force-feed most suitable for him, until, finally one day he sat up, asked for a normal dinner – and he was back to his former self, which, of course, was not what we term "normal", but, to poor Michael, was the most tolerable.

I could see Ronald writing away in his notebook.

Carrying on to the conclusion of my little tutorial, I pointed out to Ronald the amazing thing about mental illness. In my thirteen odd years as a nurse, taking me through every ward in the psychiatric hospital, covering drugs, alcoholism, all types of schizophrenia, manias, depression, epilepsy, and personality disorders, one vital factor came out, a factor which sometimes made a mockery of eminent psychologists in their theories about mental illness.

The factor was, that so many patients "knew" every phase of their illness. Michael Frost thanked me for choosing the best food for him, and my whispering condolences. He *knew* all the time what he was doing! I had a very bad schizophrenic patient, who, always behaved hysterically at the sight of snooker balls. As he was getting better, he called me into his side room, then, told me that the snooker balls represented soldiers heads.

In the case of hypo-mania, I nursed a lovely old boy, Reg Winter. As he came "down" from his manic exploits, he would talk in a serious vein, about the loss of his job, caused through his abnormal behaviour. The heart-ache he caused his wife and family. It seemed that he was trapped inside a gold fish bowl, just existing, but able to look out at the world.

Now, for the psychopaths! Who, presumably burn out at thirty. The reason for his behaviour, is, that his brain cells have not matured, that, at least, was the result, by American research experts. By the time he's forty, maybe, he'll have the brains of a genius. But, let's not knock the Consultants, or, the psychiatrists that do a grand job. It must be galling when the patient says "I knew what was happening all the time". What is the answer? Drugs treat the symptoms? But, who, treats the cause?

Ronald thanked me for my help, and wished me every success with my next book. Giving him a copy of "Dew on my feet." In like manner, I wished him success with his thesis.

During my talk with Ronald, I felt little pangs of misgiving. Making sweeping statements about mental illness, is, although I am an R.M.N., like skating on thin ice. There are so many books about the unfortunate malady, each with a different theory, each at times written by non-nursing authors.

As a nurse in charge of a geriatric ward of thirty old demented patients, I felt quite justified in writing an article to the Nursing Mirror, explaining how nurses managed to cope in feeding, bathing, and making the psycho-geriatric as happy as possible. I explained the little ruses we had to employ to enable us to cajole the old dears to take a bath, go to bed, and put on warm clothing. The demented, senile patients, mostly, fight against everything for their good – just as do small children, when having their hair brushed, or, washed, scream at mummy!

The article was accepted.

In letters to the Editor, in a later edition, most letters agreed with my disclosures. But, one stood out as a sore thumb. It was written apparently by a nursing teacher, who, disagreed with almost everything I wrote, but, giving no alternative remedies. I wrote back, to point out, that everyone is entitled to their own opinion. But, as she had signed her name with about ten different nursing courses achievements, I, guessed she had spent more time in school, than in the sluice of a hard working geriatric ward. In fact, I wondered, whether she had ever entered a sluice, since her training days. That was the end of the matter.

One can be sure that writing stories, or articles, someone is ready to shoot you down. It means of course a writer must make sure of his facts. It's amazing how on my book selling sessions I find relatives of those who I've written about. One day at a door, I was confronted with a pleasant young woman. Her first words were "You wrote about my mother in your latest book, she wants to see *you*!"

Her mother lived in an old peoples' flat a few doors away. With a little trepidation, I knocked her door. The mother came to the door in a bad mood, the daughter may have phoned her up to warn of my approach? "So you're Mr. Unwin, are you, you mentioned my name, didn't you?"

I smiled back at her, knowing that I had nothing to fear, my mention of the good lady in my book, had nothing adversely to say about her. "Yes, but I spoke only well of you – why do you seem agitated?"

The old dear, seemed surprised, that I had not made a humiliating apology and, thrown myself at her mercy. "Well, that's true. But why did you write about me, I'm just an ordinary woman, I thought books were about rich people, or people, who had done great things?"

"You *have* done great things, you brought up a big family. They all turned out honest, and hard working, one of your daughters, married a true character in my book, he was a near-blind cripple, and your daughter brought him happiness!" (His name was George Pope.)

I really meant that! The saying "Be honest, work hard, and know your place" of Oscar Wilde, had permeated through the ranks of the working class, the old lady really felt she had no right to be in the public eye. As great a figure that Oscar Wilde was in the literary world, it was incongrous, to that of his social life, thus, his sayings concerning the lower classes, were meaningless.

My intentions, in respect of my writing, was to give a little prominence to such as the old lady and her daughter!

"You'd better come in for a cup of tea, it's cold out there!" She moved aside, to allow me through the hall into the kitchen. A picture of her daughter Sue, who, had married George Pope, the crippled musician, was in the hall.

"I'm sorry I was hasty, my Sue was a good girl, wasn't she? Never thought anyone would *ever* write about my Sue. Went to the Sally Army, never missed a week, did my Sue!"

I was pleased that I'd written about Sue Previtt, why shouldn't she be written about? George Pope, had a gramaphone mounted on an old pram. The only record he had in his stock was "Colonel Bogey", as he played it to the busy shoppers, they dropped pennies into his hat. George lived in a pokey little house. When Sue came into his life, she cleaned up the house, helped him to and from his pitch – then to the pleasant surprise of the whole area, Sue married him.

The little church of St. Matthews, was filled to a flowing capacity. Surpassing many elite characters of the City, who, had married there!

Mrs. Previtt, shook hands with me as I left her flat. When I looked back, she stood at her gate, waving to me.

CHAPTER 17

The New Estates

I had now been travelling around, all over Cambridgeshire, during my dedicated role, to write, publish, and sell door-to-door, the majority of my books. Many changes had taken place. In small villages, new private estates had sprung up like mushrooms. Young couples, were selling their small houses for large sums, making a handsome profit, then, after careful "shopping around" they buy another house, the profits from the two deals, enough to build an extension on their new property, then, of course, the spiral begins all over again. One young lady, who, had that very morning, received an assessment from her surveyor on her present house, told me, she had made, in six-months, a handsome profit of sixteen thousand pounds. They were now busily building an extension to make further profit.

But it wasn't all beer, and skittles!

Being invited into hundreds of homes inside a week, I was able to listen to many of the complaints, coming, in the main, from couples, who held great store on home life. To them, a home, was like, Vera Lynn's latest song, "A house with love in it!" They wanted to settle down, bring up a small family, just, as their parents did.

The housewife, was saying "You must put this in your next book, it might help a lot of couples like me!"

She then pointed out the disadvantages of moving onto a new private estate:

People should check before taking over their "dream house". "For Sale" signs, *can* be a bad omen!

It means, usually, that "do-it-yourself" enthusiasts have moved in. D.I.Y., is a grand innovation, saving young newly weds, a good deal of money. But, it does nothing for a good night's rest, or a peaceful evening watching the telly, or, a restful afternoon.

It's bang-crash-wallop, electric drills, pneumatic hammers, and buzz-saws the order of the day. A "grannie" extension (that's the latest) or, extension to the garage or, extension to the dining room. A barbecue for the garden, new patios, a nice little brick wall all round the house, maybe, a new roof to the garage, and it's a *must*, for a brand new outhouse, for sun bathing cum – grapevines.

Now all this entails, work in the afternoon, (shift-workers) work in the early morning, 9 a.m. start (night workers), all day work (day-off) and when a week's holiday crops up, all hours, and every day. Any established resident, living either side of the D.I.Y. workaholic, gets no peace at all. Throw in the gas-fitter, the plumber, it's enough to give the Noise Abatement officer, a headache.

Then, of course, there's the domestic scene. A dirty great cement-mixer stuck outside the house for weeks on end. (Where do they get the money?) On a hot summer day, a fine film of cement dust permeates through to the washing on the line. Should that miss, you can rely on the smoke from the debris burning fanatics, to make up for any loss of discomfort. Crying babies, squabbling kids, all go to make life on a new private estate adventurous to live in, to say the least!

My informant, went on. "I'd advise any house purchaser to check up on the surroundings, watch out for the warning signs which I have touched upon. If possible, try to get onto an established estate, where the would-be home improvers have shot their bolt, and, have grown up families, sitting back on their laurels, with a nice cosy sign on the front gate "Dun-Romin!""

Returning home, I received a telephone message from "Scoop" Wilson. His old housekeeper, had returned to the fold, telling me that "Scoop" had had an accident on his Phillips scooter, broken his arm, and would I come round and see him.

The housekeeper, a Mrs Vera Day, let me in, to find "Scoop" sitting up in bed, drawn up close to the window. Vera, immediately put on the kettle, and a wink from "Scoop" consolidated all he'd told me, of lost hours of writing, through endless cups of tea!

"Thanks for the St. Neots write-ups. I did well out there, specially with the paper-peddlers; seems they aroused a good deal of attention. I broke my arm as you can see, I'd like you to do a job for me, finish off a little script for me, so's I can get it away by the week-end?"

I nodded agreement, glancing at the script, I could see it was well within my capability, poor old "Scoop's" arm, luckily, had given up the ghost, only, after the master had done most of the spade work on his St. Neots project, leaving me with just the loose ends to tie up. Not being able to type, and "Scoop's" arm injury preventing his doing do, Mrs Day came to the rescue. "My daughter's at the 'tech', she's doing well with her typing, why not come round, I'm just off anyway?"

Leaving "Scoop" gazing frustrated out of the window, I took Vera up on her invitation.

Vera's daughter Carol, was busy with her homework, as I walked into the little Council house front parlour. Her mother, looking across admiringly at Carol, beckoned me into the kitchen supplying me with the inevitable cup of tea. Looking through the window out into her garden, I spotted the usual format of the working classes idea of an ideal set-up for gardens.

A little shed, right at the bottom, with a window pointing at the house. A small chimney pipe, bending into a second-hand tortoise stove. Here, father spends cold winter mornings, mending the family footwear. A cut down motor tyre, shaped, in order to fit onto a small boy's abused tin-can kicking boots, lies next to the little hob-iron. Woolworth's 6d stick-on-soles for the better type of family shoe, still, in their unwrapped packets, there to view.

Mrs Day, a little impatient at my star gazing through the kitchen window, broke by reverie.

"I had my eyes on Mr Wilson. His housekeeper, for some years, I was. But, you writers, walk around with notebook in hand, never seem to look beyond your nose, but, your minds, are all over the place – like a butterfly, really!"

"What happened with your romance, and how come, all this?" I asked, looking at the nice cosy kitchen.

"Old 'Scoop', as you call him, wasn't the marrying type, he liked me about the place, you know, but, was just as happy, when I was away! I could see there was no chance of my hooking him. Carol's mum died, her dad was an old friend of my school days, you could say, we were meant for each other. So we got spliced, I realised how nice it was, to have a ready-made home to take over!"

The little home was reasonably furnished, in the front parlour, the usual piano, the side-board, on which stood the sepia family photographs. Straight back wooden chairs, a plant stand in the front window, on the springy floor boards, a cheap print lino insulated against wear, by a few mats in strategic places.

Vera laughed at my studying the furniture so intently. "Getting material for a story, eh? By the way, I didn't tell you how I came to be at "Scoop's". A little extra money comes in handy, I was passing, when they brought him back in the ambulance. Old "Scoop's" a good 'un. Always pays for what you do. Things, aren't too good, for me in the money stakes, what with Carol at the tech', Bert, my hubby doesn't earn much! I can always use an extra bob or two!"

I knew a little about Vera's way of coping. It was a similar way I knew of, in my own family. Dad brought home the wages on Friday night.

Pocket money was given to the child, one-penny, to last until next pay-day. Next, the rent money was placed between the folds of the rent-book, 10/- usually, Voucher money to buy clothes on the "never-never", sixpence for the Light Blue, sixpence for the Provident.

Shed interior where 'Bert' mends the childrens shoes

Ten shillings would be placed aside, for redeeming whatever had been placed in pawn, maybe, a pair of sheets, overcoat, shoes, or even the Sunday suit. All these articles had to be kept in reasonable condition, otherwise, the pledge money would be reduced.

The baker, who delivered bread to the door, he too, had to be paid. So just as the Chancellor of the Exchequer, juggles *his* money about, to look as though he's coping, Mums do a similar thing!

In accordance to whatever was needed the most, the poor harassed mum, would pay, say, the rent one week, and the baker the other, the rest she'd juggle about by sending a few rags round to George Wheatley, or, doing an odd job for someone living in a better off neighbourhood.

The funny thing about all this, was a well known saying doing the rounds in the poorer households, "If you can't pay one week, you can't pay another!"

Women, who make this remark a part of their philosophy, went about their weekly economy, as though, they, really, were carrying it out. But, deep in their hearts, they knew full well, it was a sham; I don't think I ever remember my mother ending up her weekly account, breaking even, it was a pawnshop, or else!

Vera, was looking at me in a questioning manner. "I know what you're thinking – what's in it for Carol, what's in it for me? Well, I reckon, I've sort of had my chips. When I left school, I had great hopes, I'd done well, passed my scholarship, but my people couldn't afford text books – so, it was into service. When, I first met "Scoop", it was a kind of vicarious association, "Scoop" would do, what I'd loved to have done when leaving school – but it wasn't to be!"

"And, Carol?"

"Although, she's not my real daughter, I love her as my own. I want for her, exactly what I wanted for myself. I can live my life through Carol, even better, because I won't let her make the same mistakes as myself!"

Vera, brought to my mind a true story, I'd read in my nursing days, it was featured in the "Nursing Times" or the "Nursing Mirror", and sent in by a family G.P.

One day, he was surprised to find in his waiting room, a girl of eleven, beautifully dressed, full of vibrant health, beside her, sat her mother. The woman was dressed as a tramp. She was thin, haggard, and looked an abject picture of misery, but, every time she looked at her daughter, a mother's radiance shone out.

"And what can I do for you, I see by your card that you are new in this area?" asked the G.P.

To his great astonishment, the mother asked his advice, on, when she should cease breast feeding her child?

On examination of the mother, the doctor saw that the woman was still producing milk, albeit, watery, it *was* milk. Still astounded, the doctor eventually got from the mother the full story!

Her childhood had been pathetic. She was ill-treated by both her parents. Kept, ill-clothed, poorly fed, and was sent from one children's home to another. She managed, somehow, to get married, but, she was an all-time loser, the husband turned out as cruel as her parents, and with her one child of the marriage, she left him to take up a job as a housekeeper in a live-in post, she was able to keep her daughter with her.

From then on, she decided to give her daughter everything she had been unable to procure for herself. This was taken to a degree, that bordered on insanity. She scrimped to buy her daughter the best clothes, the best food, and everything a young girl yearned for, to stop breast feeding she considered was neglect. It was a case the G.P. had never before experienced, thus, his story to the nursing journal.

I asked Vera, "Thank goodness you won't have to scrimp too much for Carol. What do you want her to do?"

Mrs Day shrugged, "As long as she takes full advantage of what's been offered her – she can't do more than that. Should she get married, I hope she chooses the right man. Anyway, I've had good talks with her, and warned her what to look out for!" with a smile, she added, "You men!".

In the meantime, Carol had finished off the typing for "Scoop". I went back to his flat, he seemed a little down. He was pleased with my work, after his perusal, I slipped it into an envelope ready for postage.

Walking past "Scoop's" little shed at the back, I noticed his battered old scooter, it lay crumpled on its side. I wondered if he had insured it, maybe, "Scoop" would manufacture a story out of it!

Amazingly, I'd read a story that very day in my local rag. A man, with a scooter similar to "Scoop", on its breaking down, decided to push it to the nearest garage, a few hundred yards away.

As, he was walking along the side of a busy road, the engine, suddenly spluttered to life.

It so astounded him, that, still hanging onto the handle-bars, he was dragged in front of an oncoming lorry, and killed. My thoughts turned to the little plots-for-the-day, and the newspaper snippets which, the correspondence courses supplied their pupils with. At the time, I was inclined to ridicule the idea, but "Scoop's" accident, bore out the fact, that, a writer must "leave no stone unturned" in order to obtain original material for his work (forgive the cliché).

Also, the old maxim, "Truth is stranger than fiction" still holds good. Who, could make up a story like that? That man could have stepped out into the road, just a yard too much, and got killed, but, for his mo-ped to burst into life, and do the job for him, certainly proves, that, truth *is* stranger than fiction.

Some writers', of course, might think all this very down market. But, the stories are slanted toward the short story market, hundreds of periodicals cater for them, and they are so easily converted into a saleable work. Say, "Scoop", on his way to St. Neots, experiences the same tragedy on *his* scooter. Mixing in the shooting at St. Neots, the bizarre episode with the paper-peddlers, you have a nice little plot for an unusual ending, maybe, the poor crazed couple, might deem it their duty to wrap "Scoop" up in their giant paper-moulds, never to be seen again! Something like the crushed car effect! Writers, *must* look to their bread and butter, lines! On my return to the hostel, I found Jenny, had been receiving letters from doting mums. One such letter had come from a couple of worried parents.

It was not unusual for Jenny to strike up a maternal type of relationship. Youngsters were leaving home for the first time, the '68s were troublesome years, drugs, anarchy, militant tendencies looked upon as the done thing. King's College, at the time was looked upon as the most liberal of colleges, as stated before, they were first to go co-ed!

As the examination term ends, results, outside the Senate House, were scoured, with agonising fervour, by students, anxious to do well, but fearful, that their pre-exam meanderings into wild parties, lazy week-ends, augered, not for parent pleasing results. Hence, the letters from parents to the hostel-keeper, in order to search for inside information. (I was already well, into my novel "In the Shadow of Kings".)

CHAPTER 18

Trouble at King's

Mr and Mrs Dixon, came to our Hostel, looking forward to a chat, and to meeting the person, who, indirectly, but in the informal way, was responsible for their son's domestice, sojourn at King's College.

Henry Dixon, had been a staunch member of the Student's Union, with rather extreme leanings to the militant left. He, also, had struck up an intimate friendship with a group intent on building up a strong following in their hippy-type "commune" brand of life style.

The idea, being, that everyone would throw in their lot as one happy unit of independent-cum-autonomic personalities. Children, for instance, in the group, would find it *not* unusual for someone other than their parents, to look after them, feed, and clothe them. In turn, they would see their parents do likewise for other children.

The motley throng could be seen climbing the Hostel staircase, to the small attic-room, let to Henry as his accommodation for the Term. They were untidy, dirty, and with deplorable feeding habits. Although scornful of everything the Social

Services stood for, they readily accepted monies from them.

Henry, once, asked for my views on his liaison with the hippy commune. I told him in no uncertain terms that you could not get away with it concerning children. An ill-child will seek comfort from its natural mother, and, what kind of mother would nurse another's child, at the expense of her own flesh blood.

Also, I told him, it would mean a break-up of the family unit, the children would suffer as they grew older, I cited my own illegitemacy as an example. All, in all, I felt it a complete disaster, with time alone, being the judge (thankfully, it all fell through).

On questioning Henry about his future when leaving college, he told me, his ambitions to become a bus-conductor, were of high priority.

Henry's parents were an elderly couple, living on the outskirts of Norwich, in a small village. They seemed worried about their son, as, they had sunk a lot of their meagre savings on furthering his education. Jenny, and I, felt sorry for them, as they sat on a sofa, in our lounge, awaiting, what we had to offer concerning their son's hope for the coming exams.

After a long discussion, before their arrival, we had decided to tell the truth about Henry's behaviour. We felt, that to build up hopes, that he might get a good degree, would be unfair, and a severe shock to them, were he to get bad marks. Mr. Dixon, however, seemed a tough nut to crack. He had complete faith in "his Henry", "a chip off the old block, is my boy, he'll do well, I know he will!"

His wife, however, in true mother tradition, as we unfolded the true goings, on, got more depressed than ever. She reiterated how they had scraped and scrimped to get Henry to King's, and how he had flouted it all in their faces.

Summoning all my psychiatric knowledge to the situation, I managed to calm Mrs. Dixon, her husband, as the truth came out, grew less flamboyant, expressing concern and comforting his wife. Jenny was a brick, she gave them tea, and promised with my help that we would have a talk with their wayward son.

There were two months to go before the Finals, so we called in Henry for tea. He seemed to sense that something was going on, apart from my previously trying to pierce his hippy connections. Jenny, minced no words. She told him, point blank, that he was slowly destroying everything his mother was doing for him. Hobnobbing, with a group of people who were willing to turn their children over to other people. Just an excuse for opting out of their responsibility. Could he not see that the children weren't being cared for, they were, dirty, poorly fed, and unhappy, they weren't being sent to school, and worst of all they watched their parents taking drugs before their very eyes.

Although I had told Henry everything Jenny had said, coming from a woman seemed more emphatic, Jenny seemed to be speaking for his mother, somehow, boys will accept chidings from their mother, sooner than a half hearted "Now, my boy, this sort of thing didn't happen in my day!" from the head of the household.

"I was looking for something different!" said Henry, a little shamefacedly, "the world seems in a terrible mess, we young people have to try and put things aright. I thought it a good thing to become independent, someone must take the lead!"

Henry Dixon – the Hippy at Kings

I looked across to Jenny and smiled.

Many students, having read a few chapters of Karl Marx, went over the top. One, such student, trying to convert me into his militant ways, which, I felt were nothing to do with Karl Marx, told me, that *everyone* should have his own business. When I asked, where the customers were forthcoming, he had no reply.

Henry, went on "My parents forced me into this, do, this, do that, they didn't expect me to think for myself. I reckoned the Commune could do something for everybody, like the Kibbutz in Israel. In any case, what was the college educating me into — !"

"But the Kibbutzs are self supporting. They work hard, they make things happen, your lot are no more than parasites. Don't the tutor's help you out in this problem?" asked Jenny.

The student smiled, "King's has a reputation for its left-wing dons, some feel the same as I do, I don't know, maybe you've got something. I get so worked up about injustice, that's why I had plans to be a bus conductor, I wanted to work my way into the Unions, become a shop steward, see what the bus-strikes were all about. On the face of it, it seems that I'm just another jerk, kicking my parents in the teeth. My old man's never done anything to alleviate injustices, just an old stick in the mud!"

"He got you thus far, into college!" broke in Jenny, "got you into Engineering, if I remember rightly – what about that, are you going to waste the degree?"

"Everyone thinks I'm skiving, but, I've been

burning the midnight oil. Anyone with an Engineering degree, must stand a good chance to work his way up in the Unions, maybe, a secretary or something – white-collar, as they call it. I may as well be an educated union-man, as just another flat-capped swaddy. I can talk to the bosses, get them a fair hearing, instead of their being flummoxed with a long word like 'margarine'."

I was, somehow, beginning to warm to Henry. Conditions at King's for the work force were terrible. Under pay, over long hours, and the cheek to call it a part-time job, in order to pay less wages, was actually our lot at King's, we were in the centre of fighting against it, with the aid of a prominent solicitor, whose premises, ironically, were opposite King's!

"Do you think you can get a decent pass in the Finals?" asked Jenny, anxiously.

Henry, smiled, "I appreciate what you're doing for me, I shall vindicate myself, in my parent's eyes. I'm confident of getting at least a 'B'. But, I'm going in for the conductor's job, I'll leave town, and go into the Midlands!"

After he'd done, Jenny and I sat musing over the events. Henry, wasn't a bad lad after all. Looking out from the rear window, we could see Tizzy's tent being hauled in by a group of young militant students. Tizzy, a real 'wow' in the militant camp, had defied King's in every aspect of their system. Fighting against rent rises, our hero had promptly placed his tent in the centre of the spacious 'quad' of the college's main entrance.

Jenny, had a lot of trouble with Tizzy in her hostel. The great man had thrown most of his belongings out of his study window onto passers by, narrowly missing a small child. Jenny, thinking that Tizzy's girl friend might have a calming effect on him, called her in, telling of Tizzy's exploits.

To Jenny's surprise, she showed little concern. Saying, "Well, if he doesn't want to own any property, O.K., by me, I feel the same away about it!"

This was the idiotic philosophy going the rounds that wicked people were possessing all the material things in life, and poor people were being crushed under. It was a complete distortion of both Karl Marx's and Christ's reasoning. *We*, were indeed, fighting for a fair wage, for a fair day's work, but, completely alien to the militant strong arm tactics.

To confirm our feelings about Tizzy, who, was sent over college after his outburst, the militant lad broke up most of the furniture in his study. We felt, caused by a mixture of amphetamines, and fool hardy politics.

To our relief, Henry managed a first-class honours degree, and after a long chat with his dad, came to an arrangement, that, he would take up an engineering appointment, with a view, that, should the occasion arise for a secretarial appointment, whereby his first love, of helping others, could be fulfilled – well, Henry would take it!

Things got hectic at the Hostel. Sit-ins, where the students crammed our one public toilet. Overfilled every dustbin with rubbish from students from other colleges. We had 100 miners, from "up North" living in the Common Room. At one stage, we thought about getting in food in readiness for a siege to take place. The whole term was a mish-mash of anarchy. Students, refused to attend lectures, on the strength that the syllabus was similar to that at Grammar School.

A student, told Jenny, "Anyway, the tutor, just stands with his back to us, scribbling on the board from a text book, held in the hand!"

Then came the Garden House fracas, a situation tailor made for the militants, involving left wing activities. The riot became famous nationally, but, the stickers, bill boards, and slogan carrying banners were manufactured in the cellars of the Market Hill hostel, our place, of course, with noise of hammers going on all night, giving us precious few hours of sleep.

Jenny, received a nice letter from Mrs Dixon, thanking us for our help, inviting us over to her's for lunch and a trip around Norwich.

Good news came concerning our right against low pay. After several consultations with the big-wigs of King's, our solicitors informed us that King's had capitulated, back pay would be forthcoming and conditions improved.

When we inquired about the cost of their service to us, they replied, "Have it on us, and should they sack you for your efforts against them, come back to us, and we'll fight for you, again, for free!"

Jenny, almost cried, to feel that the old world wasn't that bad after all.

My book, "In the Shadow of Kings" was now finished. Jenny, at times showed concern for the contents. I had told the truth about all the adverse conditions, I'd kept all documentation from our sometimes "acid" passing of mail to each other. The fact that King's spent thousands of pounds on free feasts for their students, while paying Jenny peanuts for long hours, which, they passed off as part-time, was there for all to see!

Tizzy's, and Henry's "bull-taking-by-the-horns" thoughtless skirmishes, were as nothing compared with our real grievances.

On the strength of my writing the book I received several invitations from various organisations for speeches at their functions. I did a radio interview with Carol West, and a T.V. interview for Anglia.

In each I made no bones about speaking the truth, but, at the same time, pointing out the reasons for the colleges getting away with low pay.

In the first place many Cambridge people thought it an honour to work at King's. The world-wide Carol service, the many tourists, that flocked on the place, also, T.V. programmes doing a stint on Cambridge, would find King's a must for their up-town programmes.

Then again, during the slumps of the thirties, men and women were only too pleased to have a job in a college, the money was poor, but, it was regular. Perks, were plentiful, left overs from the Provost's table, would be carried home by the bed makers and other employees.

Hostels, were usually run by a man and wife team, the man doing a job outside the college, the wife to be in charge of the hostel. The college, well knew the husband would help out his wife in onerous duties, milk-crates, dustbin carrying, and ejecting drunks or drug addicts from the hostels but, officially he was not employed there.

As accommodation was supplied by the college, the wage paid to the wife was pitiful. For being in charge of seven bed makers, responsible for furniture and bed linen, laundry listings, polish and brushes ordering, issuing keys to the students, and hundreds of other nameless jobs, Jenny, in her first week received seven pounds.

Returning from the hospital, at the time, I was nursing there, I found Jenny in tears holding her meagre earnings. It was true, we knew what the wage was going to be, little did we realise what the work entailed.

I realise now, why the ex-hostel keeper, as she handed over her keys to Jenny, burst into tears, saying "You'll regret this for the rest of your life, you'll see!"

Jenny now and again laughs at the thought of it all.

"Never mind!" she says, "You got a book out of it, so it can't be bad!"

CHAPTER 19

Appreciation

It's very nice to receive letters from abroad in appreciation from readers. It does something to an author when this happens. I always feel that a writer is as good, as his last book. Everyone likes to be praised, but, with a writer it seems a little different. You know what you've written has been well received, and it motivates you to write something even better. Here is a letter, received from a Mr John Reynolds, M.C.L.S. from Stompetowe, N. H. Holland.

Dear Mr Unwin, I see from the current issue of "The Conduct" that you have written another of your delightful books, namely "Cambridge as War Clouds Roll By". I enclose my cheque for £2.10 for same. At the moment I have the following of your works, "Pimbo", "Dew on my Feet" "Gentle Tales of Old Cambridge", "Pimbo and Jenny in Old Cambridge", and would be grateful for a copy of any missing numbers, even, if they are second hand. Signed John Reynolds.

Another ran, from Mrs N. A. Banford, Horsham.

Dear Mr Unwin, "Pimbo", has been a marvellous tonic. Having read it to my son, he is now at the age of seven, reading it again, for himself, a second time. Best wishes.

Yet another from Mrs A. Foulger, Streatham.

Dear Mr Unwin, How I enjoyed your book, I sat and read it in my garden, my husband has just finished it, too. I was so pleased you remembered my dad! Yours sincerely.

From Mrs O'Hare, Cambridge.

Since my father died recently, we have been reading your books of which he was very fond. I would like to purchase copies of all your books to date. Best wishes.

From Mrs Lawrence, Lode, Cambs.

When you called last time on your round, I was out of cash, and you kindly left the book with me. Please receive enclosed cheque for same, the book was fantastic, and I'm looking forward to your next. Best wishes.

From Rev. E. H. Bowen, Llanelli.

Your book "A Magic Book for Cats" gave me great pleasure. You must have a great imagination, to be able to intelligently write a book of that kind. It is a great work, and should give a good reading to many people. It could be a plot for a film script. Best wishes.

I have scores, and scores, of such letters in similar vein, besides, many telephone calls, that touch on the same theme. The happy feature, is, that many of these customers, have proved to be, quite happy for someone to call on them, with a book worth reading. My lingering doubts, when first tackling door-to-door selling, were soon dispelled after receiving such appreciation through letters and phone-calls.

Several people, who, were out when I called, have phoned to say "You have been round my place, sorry, I was out, can you bring me a book round?"

Of course funny things happen on my rounds. One young mother, to make ends meet, had to go out to work. She had an aged mother, who, lived a little distance away whom, she asked for me to call on as I passed, "Just to check up, Mr Unwin!"

As I entered the old dear's house, there was a terrific smell of gas, the old lady was hunched over an unlit gas fire, with it hissing away, as was the gas oven, and gas ring doing likewise.

It seems that the old lady went round each piece of gas equipment with the idea of lighting them up on cold days for warmth.

In her dementia, she *never* had a match with her, but, would still turn on the gases, with the intention of fetching her matches to finish the work. But, once back to the lounge, she forgot what she'd done, leaving the danger of gas explosions all over the house.

Ironically, her first words to me were, "Are you the gasman, have you got a match?"

Of course, I briefed her daughter about the danger her mother was now getting herself into, and she made other arrangements for the poor old lady. It could be that some kind neighbour would light the gases, without thinking about the danger, so, the daughter was the last one to find out.

At another call, I was met at the door, by a dressing gowned, rather heavily made up woman of about sixty. "Oh, I wonder if you could do something *for* me, my husband's gone out and forgotten to get it in for me. I want a bottle of whisky?" thrusting a fiver into my hand, she closed the door.

Although a little sceptic about it all, I did as she had bid, and trotted up to the pub, which, was a little way up the road.

Giving in my order, to a barman, as I spoke, the landlord put his head round the door at the rear of the bar. "Don't let her have any more Bert, that's her third today, her husband, will kill me!"

It turned out that the woman was a severe alcoholic, who, cajoled trades people to fetch her illicit cravings. When I returned to the house, I received a torrent of abuse – in fact, she was lucky to get her fiver back!

Another lady, at my knock at the door, would shout, "Come in!" Inside the kitchen, frizzling merrily on the stove, usually, stood a pan full of frying chips. Then, came a voice from the sitting-room where, she was sat, reading a journal, with the command "turn the chips, as you come in!"

After buying my book, and as I was about to take my leave, she would say "Turn the chips again, as you go out, if they're nearly done, turn down the gas!"

I found out afterwards, that, the milkman, baker, tallyman, and insurance-man, all suffered the same fate. It was a kind of black-mail, really, one refusal, and you needn't call again.

A pleasant surprise was at a house I called at in the country. Again the clarion call "Come in!" took me into the sitting-room. The place was littered with straw, hens were cackling away on the table in the centre of the room, through the open back door, came in a duck, which jumped on the lap of the lady of the house. As the hen jumped from the table, I noticed an egg had been deposited upon the tea-cosy nearby. Tiny, specially bred bantams, were picking gaily at any bread crumbs or tasty titbit to be had, they were in and out at the drop of a hat.

A large goose, with a kind of splint on its leg came hopping through the back door, took one look at me, then did a Hopalong Cassidy on me.

The lady of the house, was a large pleasant faced woman, with a lovely rosy complexion. "I know what you're thinking, but don't!" She laughed at my surprised look. "As you can see, I'm an animal lover, but, I do it in a professional manner. I run a small menagerie in the town. I collect all injured pets, in the barn, outside, I've got a crippled donkey, a one-legged duck, broken winged bats, I get kiddies coming round on their holidays, they love the place, they wash all the dirty pets, and keep my barn within the acceptance of the R.S.P.C.A.'s inspectors.

"And if you wonder why I'm sitting down doing nothing, well, it's "lap" time. All my small creatures come in at a certain time, they jump on my lap, to get a cuddle, then away they go!"

Before leaving, I took a final look around the yard, lovely capon hens, with furry gaiter-type legs, a beautiful peacock with a limp to tarnish it's dignity. Doves flapped against the top of the barn, and a tawny owl eyed me with wide eyed amazement – a truly, lovely feast of God's creatures!

Of course, I had to limit my stay in accordance to the amount of books I'd sold. Many times, I would loved to have stayed longer. One grand old man of eighty odd years, held me up quite extensively. He insisted on showing album, after album of his dear departed ones. He'd been a carrier in his early days, taking and bringing back people into town for their shopping jaunts.

Each year, as I approached his house, I wondered whether he would still be around. He cooked lovely apple-pies for himself, grew beautiful vegetables, but, the fatal day came, when, I saw the scaffolding up at the front of the house, the double glazing van outside, and that awful feeling I sensed, when a death of a customer had occurred.

Another clue to the original occupant's death, might be the daughter, now married, coming to the door, with the worry of a mortgage now in the background.

Strange people I came across at times. I used to call on a young woman's mother with my brushes. With the daughter now married, I found the young woman a delightful customer. She regularly purchased a book, especially one, where I had mentioned her dear mum!

One day, she came to the door with an evident sign of pregnancy – in fact, I felt that birth could have taken place at any moment.

As I took the money for my book, I remarked. "The best of luck my dear!" at the same time unwittingly glancing at her tummy. The result was explosive "Don't you ever call at my door again – disgusting, wishing me the best of luck – disgusting!" The woman could hardly contain herself.

Moving away, I couldn't believe that anyone could act in that way. I'd known her for years, knew her mum and dad.

With my psychiatric training to fall back on, I could only presume that either, she, or, her husband, were prudes of the very first degree. One of them, must have been brought up by people that covered up piano legs. And like the two old paper hoarding sisters, handed the neuroses over to the other's partner!

Old people cause a good deal of merriment. Mind you, it must be laughing with them, and not at them! They forget things, say ridiculous things at one moment and quite lucid things another. One old dear, whom, I'd traded with for years, both in brush and book, was showing signs of senility. After calling me in, seemingly quite lucid, purchasing my latest book, and showing me the whole set she'd bought off me over the years, she invited me to a cup of tea. While drinking the tea, the old dear looked at me quizzically "You know Mr. Unwin is such a nice man!". Then in a quick double-take, added ". . . by the way, do I know you, I get so many strange callers nowadays?".

When this happens, I pay no further calls, because it is little short of conning a person.

The overwhelming type, can at times be amusing. They call in their neighbours for a chat, while there, a knock at the door ensues.

Many times, of course, I recognise the person as not being the actual resident. The conversation usually goes "No, not to-day, thank you, the lady's busy!"

"Lap time" with the animals

I put in, "But, she doesn't know it's me, she usually buys a book, she gets cross if I miss her!"

The mediator then turns, a trifle red faced, and bawls out "You *don't* want a book do YOU?"

"Who is it, Gladys?" comes the reply.

"It's that fellow, who, writes about old characters!"

"Oh, don't let him go, I want his latest book!"

A red faced interfering old —? retires to the back of the hall. Of course, it doesn't always end that way, but, I can honestly say, in more times than not, it ends in my favour. The main reason is, that, I know the interloper, and a year goes by before I see my real customer again, and also, I respect her for liking and buying my books.

Another little ruse, played by an anti-Unwin fan, is to say "You won't find her in next door." With a cycle leaning against the wall, I give a knock anyway, and, hey-presto the customer comes to the door. This trick is never attempted by any person, other than someone who has never purchased a book from me!

I see strange notes for the milkman "On milk today" I've never fathomed out how that one came about! Then another gem. "No milk today, or Monday, Tuesday, or Wednesday – then, no more milk until further notice".

A real little cracker. "As I now have a baby, will you please start me on sterile milk from today, Thank you!"

Getting back to books, I actually feel ashamed to write anything adverse about all the thousands, and, thousands of people I call upon. Ninety-nine per cent of them are wonderful. One lady, anxious to purchase a book from me, actually, drove down to the bank while I waited at the door for her return.

The law of average, is of course, bound to lead me to a door where everything is not perfect.

As I approached a certain house, where I knew children lived, a piercing scream, followed, by outrageous threats to some hapless child rent the air. I waited before knocking until peace prevailed. A nice little mother came to the door, a sweet smiling face greeted me. As I was selling "Pimbo", her youngsters were of an age where they could enjoy it. The mother promptly bought it.

With the sale closed, I moved to the next door, but, from the house I'd just left came the same soul piercing scream – poor mum, was no doubt longing for the school holidays to end.

Another little gambit, is for the woman at the door, who, I usually remember has never yet bought a book from me, will say "Oh, my niece in so-and-so, always gets one from you, she lets me have it, when she's read it!"

I can't resist, and I only do this when I'm certain the customer *never* intends to buy a book, I say. "Oh, good, I'm glad you enjoy them let's see, how many have you read of mine to date?"

This usually throws them for six. "Oh, let me see!" they stammer "Two, I think it must be!"

As I've now written eight, I'm able to add. "Oh, you're niece must have missed me for quite a time, because, you have missed out on six!" This remark usually gets the door closed quicker than it might, allowing me to meet the genuine, good old fashioned "No".

And while I'm about it, I'd like to say to any person, who finds it difficult to deal with doorstep salesman, just say "I'm sorry, I can't honestly afford it, No!"

No salesman will waste time when he knows the customer can't afford it – if he does, well, he's flogging a dead horse!

There's no need to waffle, make excuses, because believe you me, they are easily seen through, a good old fashioned "No" works wonders!

CHAPTER 20

The Public Lending Right

I suppose should I ever write a song about myself, I would entitle it by stealing a march on Frank Sinatra, and call it “My Way”.

I didn’t dream for one moment, that I would be able to write twelve books, travel for twelve years door-to-door, and sell over 65,000 books.

You may call it what you will, self-styled vanity author, self-styled vanity publisher, but my Society of Authors’ credentials, proved otherwise.

I’ve written this book in order to help others, who, like me, aspire to be real live authors.

Now, I’m not suggesting, for one moment, that a lot of authors, would be capable of going from door-to-door as I did, and sell as many books. But what I am saying, is, that a lot of people are capable of writing books, that can go through the shops in the ordinary way, or, they can write stories good enough to be accepted by the hundreds of periodicals going the rounds, or, they can emulate dear old “Scoop” Wilson and supply articles and news snippets to hungry news journals.

Writing is, of course, a very tough medium, you have to really mean business. I came across people, who, tell me that they have written autobiographies, and they've stayed dusty, and yellow in the attic drawer.

I know an author, who has had two novels accepted, scores of articles, but, still has thirty, or so, unpublished novels stashed away.

One of *the* greatest achievements in my writing career, came through the medium of the Public Lending Right Department. In a snippet of information from the Society of Authors, own Journal, the Author, it relates that of some 11,000 registered authors eligible to receive payment, 75% of authors received less than £100. This accounts for the payment for books going through libraries from 1984–1985. To my great surprise, I received £256 made up from the following statistics:

	Loans		**Earnings**
"Dew on my Feet"	806	earned	£10.24
"From Cambridge One and All"	1,613	earned	£20.49
"Gentle Tales of Old Cambridge"	5,485	earned	£69.66
"In the Shadow of Kings"	4,517	earned	£57.37
"Knock on any Door"	161	earned	£2.04
"Pimbo"	1,129	earned	£14.34
"Pimbo & Jenny"	3,710	earned	£47.12
"What Pimbo did Next"	2,742	earned	£34.82

TOTAL SUM : £256.08

Remember "Pimbo" and "Dew on my Feet" are still going through after 12 years in circulation. The price paid for a copy going through a library is 1.02 of a penny.

Trying to be as modest as possible, this puts my books up into the 25% bracket of all registered authors. I'm pointing this out for the benefit of those would-be authors who, think it can't be done, also, to cock a snoop at the critics who say "not up-market enough". The true criticism of a writer is, the number of readers who read his/her books, not what quality newspaper critics have to say. Counting the above books of mine going through the libraries, with those I've sold door-to-door, plus, people lending them to neighbours, it makes an approximate figure close on 100,000 books going into the homes.

For those interested here is a résumé of the Public Lending Right history, as given by the Society of Authors. As it is now seven years since the passing of the P.L.R. act, and four years since the P.L.R. scheme took effect (good old politicians, three years in the wilderness) it is a good time to take stock:

- On the whole the scheme is working well.
- A few initial flaws, which, have now been removed.
- The relatively small sample of libraries introduces an element of rough justice, but is cancelled out by keeping administration to a minimum level.
- The main problem is funding. With the present mania, if it moves, cut it, may mean less money coming in, and the P.L.R. budget will continue to fail to keep up with inflation, just as sales of books to libraries and schools are falling dramatically.
- The number of authors and books is rising all the time. As the P.L.R. allocations have not been altered, the next payment to authors in February will be much lower.

- P.L.R. is statutory right not a state subsidiary, the money paid out is properly earned by writers for the extensive use made of their books.
- In relation to population, ours is the worst funded of the nine national P.L.R. systems
- Well under 10% of the Fund goes to successful and famous writers, such as; Barbara Cartland, Jeffrey Archer, Jilly Cooper, Claire Rayner, etc. 90% goes to authors whose need is real.
- P.L.R. has been paid to authors and illustrators in Australia since late 1974.

This of course is very gratifying, and I owe a lot of course to Jenny, who, has stuck by me through thick and thin. To the Burlington Press, which has produced an excellent book for me, and, of course, the illustrators, Janet, Sarah, Carol, Frances and Gwent.

The happiness derived from these successes, turned a little sour on the news that dear old "Scoop" Wilson had died. While Vera was on a two-weeks' holiday, poor "Scoop" was found dead in bed – it seemed that he'd been dead for at least a week.

Among his belongings, were several cheques from various newspapers, and journals, payment for his St. Neots disclosures. A commission to write a column on the paper peddlers, with their great mounds of paper, was by his side.

Poor old "Scoop" almost died with his boots on, he'd made arrangements that his new scooter, bought from his insurance money was to be delivered by Hallen's on the very day of his death.

Our sojourn at King's came to its end. Jenny's arthritis was not improving, we were both at pensionable age, so we decided to call it a day.

The changes we had brought about, would be most beneficial for the incoming caretakers. We held no grudge against King's, after all, they paid up in the end. Jenny misses the bedmakers' little chats in the kitchen during tea-breaks.

Farwell Scoop!

From there we gathered all the gossip on whom, was going out with whom. The old hostel was undergoing massive overhaul. Scaffolding, costing £100 per day, stood proudly outside the window. It was from the scaffolding that I actually came face to face with Peter Cook, the Cambridge rapist, who, fooled the police for so long.

The planks running across the scaffolding's iron supports, were very springy, anyone walking across them, would set up an unmistakable sound, which, told of an intruder walking up to the study windows of the students.

The students had strict orders not to climb the scaffolding, as, it was final exam's week, the rule was not likely to be broken.

It was round about 5 a.m. when I heard the sound of the springy planks. My bedroom window looked directly out onto the scaffolding, so I opened my window to look out.

Just about to enter the study window, next to mine, was a small chunky figure, wearing gloves. Not knowing at the time, that this man was the actual rapist, I'm afraid I allowed him to completely fool me.

Holding his fingers up to his lips, as though he was about to commit a playful prank, and, didn't want me to give him away, I foolishly smiled back, and forgot the incident.

Later in the day, there came one complaint after the other. The student next to my room had lost a watch and radio. Several other students had similar articles taken from their rooms.

The police, quickly sussed out the man responsible, as the very elusive Peter Cook, who, went on to terrify girls in bed sitters and hostels all over the City. Cook, had the effrontery to leave his trade mark behind, by writing slogans on the dressing table mirrors, usually with the frightened girl's own lipstick.

This terrible man was eventually put away, but, before his capture, he would be brazen enough to walk into the Police station, and ask "Have you caught the old so-and-so yet?".

I have just finished a new book, this time it was a fun book, a "send up" of the criminal fraternity of the City.

During my sojourn in the desert war, to help give the troops a little relaxation, a magazine was brought out, called "Nulli Secundus". I was asked to make a contribution, literary wise, so I invented a couple of detectives called Ivor Notion and Stonk!

It sounds pretty tame nowadays, but the troops loved it, because I used the Army as the basis for the plots, so, was able to take it out on officers, N.C.O.s and privates, alike, all in fun of course!

This, I was putting in "Cambridge Tales of Mystery and Mirth". With my vast experience of going door-to-door and cocking an ear to the "Now, I don't know how true it is – but they tell me – ?" little gems of half-true gossip.

A wages robbery at Spicer's paper-mill some years ago, had the City humming with innuendos, concerning suspects.

Lots of petty thieving, could by gossip, be brought to the door, of quite well known characters, whom, the police, although pretty sure of their guilt, had no evidence.

So, I had murders committed, scandals spreading galore, using all the mixture of half-truths and fallacy. Using, funny, snappy, surprise endings, took away any sense of malice, so I never received a letter of any complaints after its publication.

Trying to be original wasn't easy. As far as possible I avoided any reference to sexual deviations, keeping the book strictly family, allowing the school-children to be able to read it without a fear of polluting young minds.

Sometimes, a burly looking unshaven man, would flick through the pages of my book and handing it back to me, would say "Not my scene, mate!".

I knew of course, what he meant, I also knew that the type of book he wanted, sold many many more, than I could ever achieve with mine. But, that's life! In my psychiatric work, I have known patients, especially young ones, brought up in ultra-rigid puritanical backgrounds, to be so puzzled and confused by sex, that they thought "kissing" would make them pregnant!

The type of literature the "unshaven" man was looking for, was of immense help to such young patients in Fulbourn.

I knew of a spinster, as rigid as a ram-rod, who, was visited by young children collecting for Bonfire night. During the course of the hand-over of a few coins, one little chap, innocently remarked, "my cat's going to have kittens, miss!"

The reply, before the door was slammed by the disgusted "Spinster of this Parish", was "Go away, don't talk dirty!"

So, a writer must be very broad minded, without of course, condoning hard "porn".

Jenny took up knitting after her departure from the college. She knitted cardigans, gloves, pull-overs, everything imaginable. Sometimes, she'd say "I wish I could think up stories like you".

And I reply "But, your knitting *is* creative, just as clever, to follow a few purl and plain words, then produce a beautiful garment, especially when you find the actual pattern has been mis-printed!" (So you ladies knitting away in the little back street, take heart, you, too, are being creative).

One day, Jenny turned to me, and asked,

"If there's one thing you'd like to use as a tip for budding writers, what would it be?"

Thinking of my early struggles, I replied.

"Not to leave their bicycle leaning against the window, or, their lorry on the No Parking Lines, and, always, take off your cycle clips, before entering the interview room!" After all, what is fame? Fame is but a slow decay!